MANUSCRIPT PAINTING AT THE COURT OF FRANCE

THE FOURTEENTH CENTURY

MANUSCRIPT PAINTING AT THE COURT OF FRANCE

THE FOURTEENTH CENTURY (1310-1380)

FRANÇOIS AVRIL

GEORGE BRAZILLER NEW YORK

A Marie

Translated from the French by Ursule Molinaro with the assistance of Bruce Benderson

Published in 1978.

For information address the publisher:
George Braziller, Inc., One Park Avenue, New York, New York 10016

Library of Congress Cataloging in Publication Data

Avril, François.
Manuscript painting at the court of France.

Bibliography: p.
1. Illumination of books and manuscripts, French.
2. Illumination of books and manuscripts, Gothic—France. I. Title

ND 3147.A88 745.6′7′0944 77-78721

ISBN 0-8076-0878-5

ISBN 0-8076-0879-3 pbk.

First Printing
Printed by Imprimeries Réunies in Switzerland

Designed by Randall de Leeuw

CONTENTS

ACKNOWLEDGEMENTS

The author and publishers would like to express their sincere thanks to the following institutions and individuals who kindly provided materials and granted permission to reproduce them in this volume.

Color Plates

BRUSSELS, Copyright Bibliothèque Royale Albert Ier, Plate 33.

GENEVA, Bibliothèque Publique et Universitaire, Plate 14 (Photo, François Martin, Photographe).

LONDON, Reproduced by permission of the British Library Board, Plates 27, 28, 31.

LONDON, Victoria and Albert Museum, Plates 21, 22 (Photos, L. East and P. Macdonald, Photographers).

NEW YORK, The Metropolitan Museum of Art, The Cloisters Collection, Purchase, 1954, Plates 3, 4, 5, 6, 7, 8, 9, 10. The Cloisters Collection, 1969, Plates 18A, 18B, (Photos, Charles Passela).

PARIS, Bibliothèque de l'Arsenal, Plate 37 (Photo, Bibliothèque Nationale, Paris).

PARIS, Bibliothèque Nationale, Plates 1, 2, 11, 12, 13A, 13B, 15, 16, 17, 19, 20, 23, 24, 25, 26, 29, 30, 32, 34, 35, 38, 39, 40 (Photos, Bibliothèque Nationale, Paris).

THE HAGUE, Rijksmuseum Meermanno-Westreenianum, Plate 36 (Photo, A. Frequin).

Black-and-White Figures

BERLIN, Kupferstichkabinett Staatliche Museen Preussischer Kulturbesitz, Berlin (West), Figure X (Photo, Jörg P. Anders).

LONDON, Reproduced by permission of the British Library Board, Figure VIII.

PARIS, © Arch. Phot. Paris/S.P.A.D.E.M., Figure VII.

PARIS, Bibliothèque Nationale, Figures I, II, IV, V, VI, IX, XI, XII (Photos, Bibliothèque Nationale, Paris).

PARIS, Musée du Louvre, Figure XIII (Cliché des Musées Nationaux, Paris).

ROME, Biblioteca Apostolica Vaticana, Figure III.

INTRODUCTION

At the beginning of the 14th century, the arts in France displayed the same strong tendency toward centralization in Paris as was true of French politics. Such centralization was unequaled in the rest of Europe at that time. Seat of a powerful, respected monarchy and of a prestigious university whose influence extended to all of Western Christianity, Paris was destined from the preceding century to become one of the principal European centers of book production and, above all, of manuscript painting. This was so much the case that Dante, in an often quoted passage from the *Divine Comedy,* could link Paris to the "art of illumination." Outside Paris, and especially in the northern part of the kingdom, illuminators gradually lost their originality and, whether they submitted to or resisted the influence of the capital, fell for a time into provincialism.

It was in Paris, however, that the art of the future was being forged. Leaving their native regions, the best talents streamed into the capital, attracted by the rich clientele of the Court. To repeat Erwin Panofsky's image, Paris became a reservoir into which poured the vital forces of the artistic world from France, and even from the rest of Europe.

Despite the regional diversity of its artists, it would be a mistake to think of Paris in the 14th century as a Tower of Babel. The unity in style of Parisian production during that period was, on the contrary, quite striking, even in cases involving totally different techniques. This homogeneity was the result of several factors: first, Paris maintained well-established stylistic and decorative traditions, to which the newcomers promptly adapted themselves; and, second, the artists of the capital had, for the most part, come from northern France, Flanders or England where they shared a profoundly similar cultural background. Another, still more decisive factor accounting for this stylistic unity, seems to have been the refined and lofty taste of the Court whose role had been relatively discreet during the preceding century, but whose influence continued to grow during the course of the 1300s. With the development of court patronage there appeared a new type of illuminator and painter, who worked exclusively for the royal family and other noble patrons, who shared their lives and was thus freed, once he had established a reputation, from those commercial necessities which continued to dominate less talented artists, serving a less exalted clientele, i.e., the burghers and the university circles. This evolution toward what might be called the "palace artist" began with Master Honoré at the end of the 13th century, and reached its apotheosis a quarter of a century later with Jean Pucelle. As was true in other eras and other civilizations, the privileged relationship between these exceptional artists and their patrons produced a remarkable series of masterpieces, each one an essential link in the remarkable evolution French illumination experienced in the course of the 14th century.

A major factor in the flowering of European Gothic painting during this period was the work of the two leading Italian painters of the Trecento, the Florentine Giotto, and the Siennese Duccio. Their innovations—the evocation of a deeper and more functional pictorial space and the profound interpretation of human emotions and sentiments—were to eventually influence the rest of Western Christianity. They spread like a ground swell, their influence being felt first in painting within the regions bordering the Mediterranean, especially in Catalonia and Provence. In northern Europe, it was in Paris that these discoveries struck a particularly profound chord, revealing to the northern artist new possibilities for expressing his traditional love of the direct, accurate observation of nature. Still, the new art of painting germinating in Italy could not have penetrated so deeply into a milieu that was as organized and as traditionalistic as that of the Parisian illuminators (these being the only artists whose reactions to the Italian innovations can be appreciated, since the monumental pictorial legacy of that time has almost completely disappeared), if certain local conditions had not favored its introduction. These included support from political authority, attested to by the fact that, as early as 1309, Philippe IV (le Bel), King of France, employed a team of Italian painters to decorate his castle in Poitiers; and the development of the art trade, proven by the sale of paintings of "Roman workmanship," as early as 1328, to Countess Mahaut d'Artois.

These favorable, but "exterior" conditions would have been of little consequence, however, without the support of the native artists themselves. The impact of Italian painting was felt precisely at a moment when a latent need for renewal was beginning to manifest itself in French illumination. Until the end of the 13th century, French illumination had remained essentially graphic and linear in character; its pictorial realization hardly exceeded the level of colored drawings. However, a few works of that era, in particular those of Master Honoré, already displayed a new interest in the third dimension, evidenced by the introduction of

I

raised elements and skillful modelling, intended to create an impression of relief. Applied to the surface of the painted page, Honoré's figures were treated plastically but still remain inscribed within a flat and depthless space. It required Jean Pucelle's genius to bridge the next phase and introduce three-dimensional space to French illumination.

Until 1320, when Pucelle made his appearance on the Parisian art scene, two definite stylistic trends ruled illumination in the capital. The first trend was directly derivative of Honoré and continued until about the 1330s with works such as *The Bible of Jean de Papeleu,* dated 1317 (Paris, Bibliothèque de l'Arsenal, Ms. 5069), and Vincent de Beauvais' copy of the *Miroir Historial* which was probably executed shortly after 1333 for John, Duke of Normandy, the future John II of France (Leyden, Bibliothèque de l'Université, Ms. Voss. Gall. folio

3a). These manuscripts, which have occasionally been attributed to Honoré's son-in-law Richard de Verdun, are characterized by a flexible, sinuous line in keeping with the elegant Parisian productions of the second half of the 13th century. A particularly fine, little known example of this style appears in a missal executed around 1320, probably destined for the chapel of a member of the royal family. In this manuscript, the figures of the Crucifixion have been treated with a vigorous plasticity which is already remarkable, despite a certain mannerism in the poses which was a direct legacy of Honoré. At the same time, their full round faces and soft contours recall certain paintings of the Siennese school, especially the work of Simone Martini. Whether this similarity is fortuitous or not, the work remains a significant example of the climate in which the ultimate rapprochement of French and Italian cultures occurred.

In contrast to the fluid drawing style of Honoré's followers, the paintings in the famous manuscript of *The Life of Saint Denis* which Gilles de Pontoise, Abbot of Saint Denis, offered to King Philippe V (le Long) in 1317, show a striking firmness of design and solidity of form. The pose of the figures is no longer affected nor their stance exaggerated; theirs is a new monumentality and nobility of bearing. Georg Vitzthum may or may not have been right in ascribing the style of these paintings to Anglo-Flemish antecedents, but he was certainly right to consider them examples of a new trend in Parisian illumination. This trend was characterized not only by the almost sculptural treatment of the figures, which, according to the same Vitzthum, seem as though they had been carved in wood, but also by the attentive observation of daily reality, as shown in the scenes which were inserted into *The Life of Saint Denis.* These are lively scenes in which the action takes place in Lutece, depicting various aspects of commercial and artisan activities in Paris at the beginning of the 14th century. A similar turning away from the elegant standards of the Parisian tradition is discernible in a satirical work of the same period, the *Roman de Fauvel* (Figure I); the pen and ink illustrations which are heightened with color reveal an artist more interested in expressiveness than in linear refinement. It appears that this resourceful artist, who may have been a native of Artois, later directed a workshop which specialized in illustrations of historical texts and romances, many of which shared the characteristic of being divided into three columns of script.

Still, during the second decade of the 14th century, a new style appeared in several Parisian manuscripts which reconciled the emphasis on elegance of Honoré and his followers with the formal solidity toward which the painters of *The Life of Saint Denis* were striving. One example is the *Decretum Gratiani,* copied in 1314 by a scribe of English origin, Thomas Wymondswold. The best of the three artists who collaborated on the illustration of this manuscript is distinguished by a suppleness and purity of design and a clarity of composition, traits clearly heralding the art of Pucelle (Figure II).

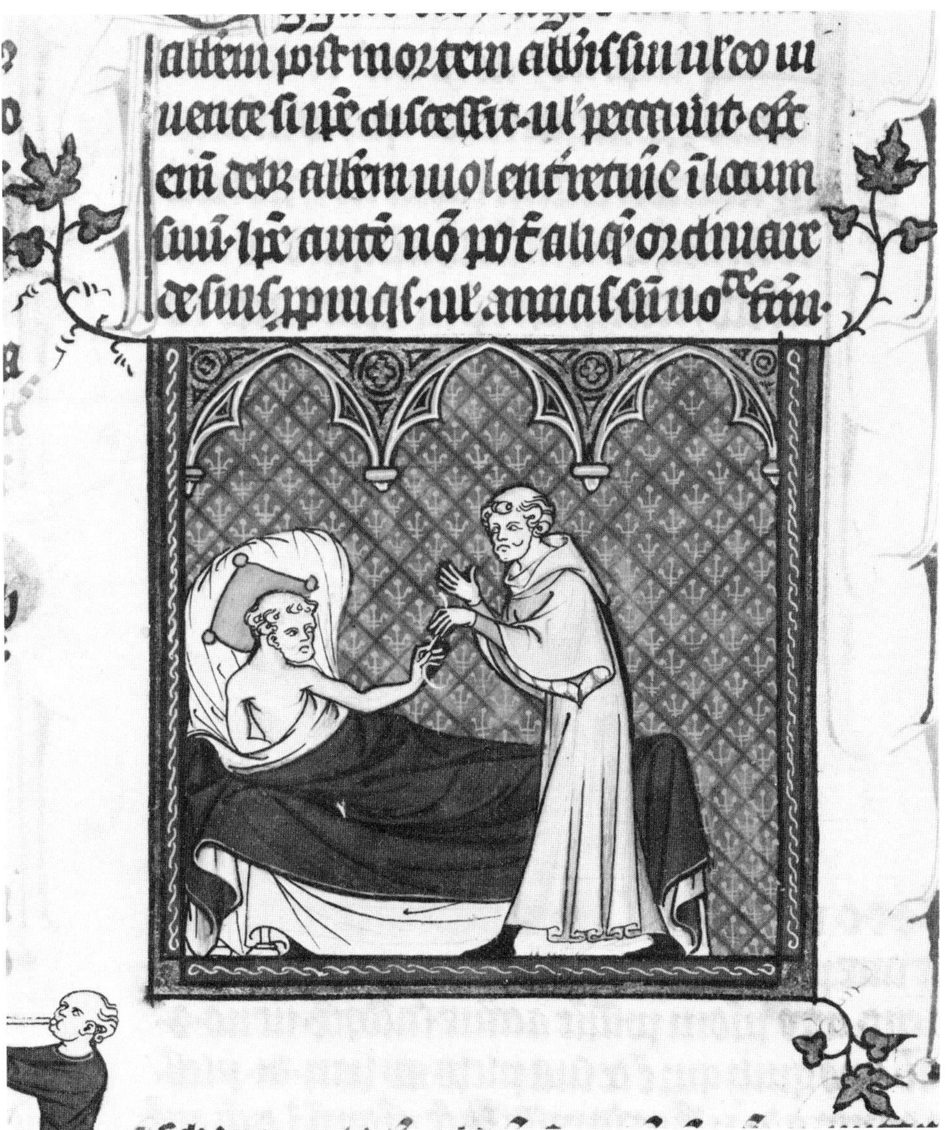

II

The earliest works attributed to Jean Pucelle hardly go back beyond 1320. Considering that the artist was dead by 1334, the deep imprint he left upon his contemporaries appears all the more remarkable. Two types of evidence agree in establishing the important role that Pucelle played in the history of French illumination during the 14th century: first, written documents, which are, for him, more numerous than for any other illuminator of the period; and second, the fact that his name is undeniably linked with the most refined and advanced works of his time. There thus appears no reason to try, as has sometimes been the case, to minimize his importance as an innovator.

Contrary to what one might expect, the oldest document which mentions Pucelle is not related to his craft as an illuminator, but concerns rather a payment made to the artist between 1319 and 1324 for the design of the grand seal of the Confraternity of the Hospital of Saint-Jacques-aux-Pèlerins in Paris. Apart from revealing Pucelle's relationship with an institution that was patronized by three of the greatest ladies of France—Queen Jeanne, the wife of Philippe V (le Long), Countess Mahaut d'Artois, and her daughter, the Duchess of Burgundy—the document is important because it shows the unusual position of an artist who, far from being restricted to decorating manuscripts, is being charged with a work that will later be executed in a different medium.

Another series of documents shows Pucelle's activity as an illuminator. There is the first inscription, written in tiny letters in red ink at the end of a luxury Bible signed by Robert de Billyng, a copyist of English origin (Bibliothèque Nationale, Ms. Lat. 11935), which informs us that the manuscript has been illuminated by Jean Pucelle, Anciau de Cens, and Jaquet Maci. Then there are tiny footnotes written at the bottom of certain leaves in the first volume of *The Belleville Breviary* (Plates 11–12), which inform us that the decoration of the manuscript had been entrusted to Pucelle who, in this case, served as the head of the team and remunerated the various collaborators who helped him realize the program. And finally, there is the wonderful Book of Hours painted in *grisaille,* kept now at The Cloisters (Plates 3–10). Although it does not mention his name explicitly, it is, nonetheless, together with the two preceding manuscripts, one of the best documented works by Pucelle. There is absolutely no reason to doubt that it is the Book of Hours "illuminated in black and white for the use of the Preachers," described in the inventories of 1401 and 1416 of the Duke Jean de Berry. Here, the manuscript is designated as *The Hours of Pucelle.* Another document, the inventory of Charles V's jewels at Vincennes, describes a very similar manuscript bound with the Arms of Queen Jeanne d'Évreux. One has every reason to identify the Book of Hours at The Cloisters both with the *"petit livret d'oraisons"* ("a very little book of prayers") bequeathed to Charles V in 1371 by his aunt, Jeanne d'Évreux, and probably with the item mentioned in the Vincennes inventory.

The article in Jeanne d'Évreux' last will and testament is doubly interesting: it clearly states that the *"livret d'oraisons"* was illuminated by Pucelle, and that it had been commissioned for the Queen by her deceased spouse, which dates its execution back to the years 1325–1328, the beginning and end of Charles IV's (le Bel) brief reign. Moreover, it can never be stressed enough how exceptional it was for an artist's name to be mentioned in the inventories of that period: that Pucelle's name was remembered almost forty years after his death in Jeanne d'Évreux's will, that his name was still being mentioned in the inventories of Jean de Berry, at a time when a pleiad of remarkable new artists had arisen, proves sufficiently how impressive he was to his contemporaries and to the generations that followed, that he appeared to them, as he does to us, as such an extraordinary artist. To comprehend Pucelle's originality we have only to examine *The Hours of Jeanne d'Évreux,* the true masterpiece of his art. It is also the only manuscript which we are certain was entirely executed by the hand of Pucelle. This cannot be affirmed either in the case of *The Billyng Bible,* nor of *The Belleville Breviary.* It is also the only manuscript in which he seems to have been able to give free reign to his creative inspiration. Everything in this manuscript surprises. First of all is its tiny format, a true *tour de force* of miniaturization; second, there is the fact that the master executed even the smallest detail of the decoration himself, without calling upon any collaborator to undertake the secondary ornamentation, as was the custom at that time; the illustrations themselves, even those in the initials and line endings—each one treated with such variety and invention—are all by the hand of Pucelle. A third point deserves to be emphasized: the manuscript is the first great masterpiece of French illumination to have been executed in tones of gray (*grisaille*), a technique which seems to have been prompted by aesthetic choice rather than by a preconception of religious austerity, and which met with lasting success throughout the entire 14th century.

These particularities are nonetheless only secondary, compared to the essential interest of *The Hours of Jeanne d'Évreux,* i.e. the stylistic and iconographic innovations which Pucelle incorporated into the illustrations themselves. First of all, from a stylistic point of view, *The Annunciation* in the Hours of the Virgin, and the *grisaille* showing the queen on her *prie-dieu* at the beginning of the Hours of Saint Louis, represent the first attempt, north of the Alps, to recreate an interior in three dimensions. Thanks to a whole gamut of subtle variations in value, combined with the usual empirical perspective, the effect of depth obtained is remarkably convincing. It is true that, at the time *The Hours of Jeanne d'Évreux* was executed (around 1325–1328), such spatial evocations were everyday fare south of the Alps, and compared to his Italian models, Pucelle's limitations are quite evident. But, nonetheless, he was the first artist in France to have taken an important step toward mastering spatial problems and thus to have helped disseminate among his Parisian colleagues a simplified and thereby accessible version of the pictorial concepts of Italian invention.

Like all great artists, Pucelle was not only a creator of form, he was also interested in evoking emotions by the scenes he represented. Here, too, he put the experience of the Italian masters to good use, as can be seen in *The Hours of Jeanne d'Évreux. The Crucifixion* scene, as well as the scene of *The Lamentation over the Body of Christ,* uncommon in France, present details of pathos hitherto unknown in northern iconography but found in compositions of Duccio: the *spasimo* of the Virgin in *The Crucifixion,* and the attitude of Marie-Magdalene wringing her arms as a sign of despair in *The Lamentation* are two such examples. Stimulated by these models, Pucelle was also able to make truly creative innovations which his predecessors would not have disavowed. The almost pagan

III

IV

nudity of the Christ Child in *The Adoration of the Magi* is a typical example. This depiction must have seemed too audacious to his contemporaries, and his followers carefully refrained from repeating it. It was not until the 1380s that this innovation reappears in the Epiphany scene.

However great Pucelle's debt to Italian art may have been, it is astounding to see with what ease he was able to incorporate these foreign influences into his own artistic concepts. Pucelle denied nothing of his original cultural heritage, and continued to emphasize clarity of expression and formal elegance as much as had his Parisian predecessors. His manner of treating religious iconography, his intimate tenderness tinged with humor, everything bears the imprint of a northern formation, amply confirmed by the enchanting grotesques strewn abundantly throughout the entire manuscript. The choice of his models is equally characteristic: to the powerfully monumental painting of Giotto he prefers the art of Duccio, whose refined style and spare forms were more readily assimilable by a northern illuminator.

Aside from *The Hours of Jeanne d'Évreux,* which may be considered his key work, one customarily divides the rest of his *oeuvre* into two groups: those which preceded his contact with Italian art—a contact which the many precise borrowings from the back of Duccio's *Maestà* indicate had taken place during a voyage to the Peninsula—and those from the artist's maturity, which can be recognized by their Italianism. Among the works of his youth, the charming *Franciscan Breviary* in the Vatican Library (Ms. Urb. Lat. 603) is particularly interesting. Pucelle worked only to a minor extent on this manuscript, destined for a Princess of royal blood, Blanche de France, daughter of Philippe V (le Long). He collabo-

V VI

rated with various artists whose style is typical of Parisian art between 1310 and 1320, especially with a follower of Honoré, an artist closely associated with the illustrator of *The Bible of Jean de Papeleu.* In the pages executed by Pucelle in the manuscript, one immediately recognizes his inimitable grotesques enlivening the margins, and his underlying interest in presenting deep space (Figure III). Besides *The Hours of Jeanne d'Évreux,* two other manuscripts are explicitly connected with Pucelle, *The Billyng Bible* and *The Belleville Breviary,* both belonging to his maturity. The appreciation of the first, dated 1327, had been complicated for a long time by the famous "signature," which indicated the collaboration of two other artists besides Pucelle, i.e., Anciau de Cens and Jaquet Maci. It has as yet not been possible to determine which part each played in the execution of the historiated initials in the Bible. As a matter of fact, each of the three artists seems to have been charged with a different task. It seems certain that Maci took care of the filigree decoration, and that Anciau, who is probably the same as Ancelot whom Pucelle paid for his collaboration on *The Belleville Breviary,* most likely limited himself to the execution of the decorative elements in the Bible (painted initials and borders). Pucelle must have reserved the *histoires*—in other

VII

words: the illustrations—for himself. With relatively little freedom in the illustration of a text which was subject to well-established iconographic rules, and despite the restricted space at his disposal, Pucelle nonetheless displayed, in various places, his interest in the third dimension, which he suggests by means of architectural elements treated in high relief (Figure IV). In *The Belleville Breviary,* which takes its name from its probable patron, Jeanne de Belleville, the iconographic program of both volumes is more ambitious and inventive. The Calendar of the first volume of this manuscript contains a cycle of highly elaborate illustrations, which combine the symbolic representation for each month with Articles of Faith, the Credo of the Apostles, and the Labors of the Month. Although only the last two months remain in *The Belleville Breviary,* the full Calendar is fortunately known to us, through several copies made as late as the beginning of the 15th century in Paris, and as far away as Catalonia. From the point of view of pictorial execution, the Breviary occupies a special place in Pucelle's works. The artist seems to have left a large part of the work on the illustrations to his collaborators (collaborators other than those whose names appear in the manuscript, charged with the secondary decoration) to whom he assigned the task of completing and painting the compositions which he had conceived. Otherwise, the difference in material execution which exists between the paintings in the Breviary and those in the other manuscripts by the hand of Pucelle would be hard to understand.

Two other works can be attributed to the end of Pucelle's artistic career, *The Breviary of Jeanne d'Évreux* (Chantilly, Musée Condé), and a luxury edition of *The Miracles of Notre-Dame* by Gauthier de Coincy (Paris, Bibliothèque Nationale, Ms. Nouv. Acq. Fr. 24541). Like *The Hours of Jeanne d'Évreux*, this Breviary, which was executed around 1330, is illustrated in tones of gray, but Pucelle shows himself to be less free of the design restrictions imposed by page layout. The work's main value consists of certain iconographic inventions. The illustrations for *The Miracles of Notre-Dame* are the artist's last important work, and show a procession of persons belonging to different classes of society who were all saved by the intervention of the Virgin (Plate 13). After *The Hours of Jeanne d'Évreux*, this is the work in which Pucelle has been able best to exploit the teachings which he brought back from his voyage to Italy. His representations of interiors are particularly successful (Figure V), and the really surprising appearance of a Tuscan citadel in one of the miniatures reveals precise knowledge of trans-Alpine architecture (Figure VI). The slightly heavy execution of certain scenes, the tones, rich and dark, accented with light in certain spots, are a new aspect of Pucelle's art, and it is possible that he belatedly adopted the techniques of easel painting. *The Miracles of Notre-Dame* ends the series of major works which may rightfully be attributed to Pucelle. Françoise Baron's recent discovery of the year of Pucelle's death (1334) imposes a reconsideration of the scope of his work and the elimination of several manuscripts which had heretofore been attributed to his final period of activity—a period that had been assumed to have continued until the middle of the century, and even beyond. Pucelle occupies an important position in the arts of his time, despite the relative brevity of his career. It is remarkable that resonances of his style appear not only in illumination, but also in various other media. An embroidered mitre in the Church of Sixt in Savoy is a striking example (Figure VII), and raises the question of whether Pucelle and his disciples were not more than once involved in designs for media as diverse as enamelling, embroidery, and even ivory, to mention only the minor arts. The example of Pucelle's model for the seal of the Hospital of Saint-Jacques-aux-Pèlerins supports this hypothesis.

Pucelle dominated Parisian art life far longer than just the first half of the 14th century. His style survived for many years after his death, thanks to an outstanding illuminator who must certainly have been trained in Pucelle's workshop, whose direction he probably assumed after 1334. This artist was the true spiritual heir of his master. He had probably saved his master's models and collections of designs. Unlike Pucelle, however, he seems to have had an extremely long career. Well before the middle of the century he had been responsible for important

VIII

TABLEAU qui est au dessus de la porte de la Sacristie dans la Ste. Chapelle
du Palais a Paris, ou est represente JEAN Roy de France.

IX

works that, heretofore, had been considered late productions by Pucelle, e.g., *The Hours of Jeanne de Navarre,* in which he illustrated the Office of the Virgin and the Office of the Passion (Plates 15–17), and certain paintings in *The Psalter of Bonne de Luxembourg,* the first wife of Jean le Bon (Plate 18).

After 1350, this artist reappeared as the creator of *The Book of Hours of Countess Yolande of Flanders* (Figure VIII), which, unfortunately, has been badly damaged. Later, he worked for King Charles V, whose *Breviary* he illuminated almost entirely (Plate 37), and for whom he also painted the initial *grisaille* for a *Bible Historiale* (Paris, Bibliothèque de l'Arsenal, Ms. 5212) of extremely elaborate iconography (Plate 38). His last works were the miniatures in *The Petites Heures de Jean de Berry* (Plate 39), probably executed around 1372–1375, when the work was probably interrupted by his death. Ten years later the illustration of this manuscript was taken up again and completed by a team of artists under the direction of Jacquemart de Hesdin.

It seems reasonable to identify this excellent illuminator as Jean Le Noir, an artist whose career presents a striking parallel with Pucelle's: a series of documents shows Le Noir successively in the service of Yolande of Flanders, Charles V, and Jean de Berry. Le Noir's appeal to the great becomes readily understandable when one examines his works. They show him as a "true reincar-

X

nation of Pucelle," to repeat Millard Meiss's well-coined expression. He completely assimilated Pucelle's style and he quite openly repeated Pucelle's most original creations almost without any modification. Twice in a row, in *The Hours of Jeanne de Navarre* and in *The Hours of Yolande of Flanders,* he and his workshop repeat the Calendar Pucelle had conceived for *The Belleville Breviary* (Plate 11), perhaps at the order of his royal clients. The psalter cycle in the same manuscript became Le Noir's model for Charles V's *Breviary.* Despite his stylistic dependence and his unmodified borrowings—of which there are a number of other examples—the artist is better than an imitator, even a talented one. Behind his apparent submission to Pucelle, Le Noir concealed a firm personality which was sensitive to the art of his time, as shown by the gradual replacing of the idealized human figures that were so dear to Pucelle by more expressive and more finely characterized figures. He excelled in scenes of violence and sometimes had a tendency to translate passion into excessive gestures, which nonetheless achieved an admirably dramatic and ornamental effect.

The exquisite sensitivity of Pucelle's and Le Noir's art corresponded perfectly to the refined tastes of the feminine and princely clientele for whom it was destined. However, from the middle of the 14th century on, conditions of artistic patronage underwent an important change. Interest in books was no longer the monopoly of Queens and Princesses. The French Kings who had remained more or less in the background until that time now began to exhibit a definite interest in books, leaving their mark upon the literary production of the period, with an emphasis on translations and the creation of new works. The first King actually to have followed such cultural policy deserving of his name was Jean le Bon (1359–1364), an unlucky monarch, whose taste for the arts and for books can be seen in many works. Even before he acceded to the throne, he had assembled an interesting collection of manuscripts, and during his brief reign he found the time to launch several important literary ventures. It was his initiative which resulted in Livy's three decades of Roman History being translated by Pierre Bersuire, as well as Jean de Sy's monumental translation and commentary on the Bible, a work that was left unfinished after the defeat at Poitiers (1356). He also commissioned a remarkable *Bible Moralisée* (Plates 19–20), which will be dealt with more extensively later because of the important role it has in the history of Parisian illumination in the middle of the century. Another captivating feature of the King's personality was the active interest he took in painting, as shown by his instructions to Jean Coste whom he had commissioned to decorate the walls of his castle in the Vaudreuil. When he was exiled to England, he took along Girard d'Orléans, who was both his painter and his valet.

Royal patronage was tragically interrupted after Poitiers due to the continuing captivity of King John, who spent most of his remaining life in England. It was taken up again on a wider scale by his son and successor, Charles V, whom his biographer Christine de Pisan has called "the wise king." From the very beginning of the regency, which he assumed in 1356, this enlightened and scholarly monarch not only began the reconstruction of France in the face of enormous political, economic, and social difficulties, but also assembled what was destined to become the richest royal library of the period. At the end of his reign, Charles V's library included nine-hundred volumes. These were distributed among various royal residences, but the major portion were divided between the Louvre and Vincennes. In addition to the books which he received as gifts, by legacy, or acquired through confiscation, his library also consisted of a considerable number of manuscripts which had been executed at the King's behest and which reveal his personal interests. Historical works, such as the *Grandes Chroniques de France,* political treatises, like *Le Songe du Verger,* translations of patristic texts like Saint Augustine's *City of God,* or philosophical ones, like Aristotle's *Ethics, Politics,* and *Economics,* liturgical compilations such as the *Rational des Divins Offices* by Guillaume Durand, an ordinary of the ceremony, recording the pageantry of Charles V's coronation in 1364, are all works which transformed the royal library into a veritable instrument of political thought, and also revived the prestige of the Valois dynasty which had suffered greatly from the defeats by England and the political crisis which had ensued. Following the King's example, his three brothers, Louis d'Anjou, Philippe le Hardi, Duke of Burgundy, and especially Jean de Berry, were also enlightened book lovers. During his elder brother's lifetime, Jean de Berry chose, with unfailing good taste, the best artists of his time to decorate his two Books of Hours (Plates 39–40).

The assumption of patronage by the masculine element of the royal family may, in part, be related to the coinciding development of a new naturalist trend in illumination which became evident during the third quarter of the 14th century. This new trend contrasted strongly with the love for formal and linear perfection manifested by Pucelle and his followers. It seemed as though the serene and idyllic view of the artists of the first half of the century was no longer valid at a time when France was experiencing epidemics and the first devastations of the Hundred Years' War. Perhaps the time had come for a new style focused on an unbiased observation of reality and nature. The human face was no longer shown exclusively according to an idealized mold of perfect proportions which had been the rule in manuscripts illustrated by Pucelle and his school. There was no longer any hesitation in showing physical imperfections, or the ugly, but individualistic features of certain personages. It was precisely at this point that the idea of portraiture made its appearance. The first preserved example of its kind (though it seems to have been preceded by older panels) is the famous portrait of Jean le Bon in the Louvre. It was rapidly followed by a large number of similar paintings in the manuscripts of Charles V (one of the French Kings whose physical appearance is most familiar to us), a fact which proves the influential role played by larger-scale painting in the evolution of illumination at that time. This search for physiognomical truth is paralleled by a new interest in current events as, for example, in the series of illustrations for *The Coronation Book of Charles V* (Plates 27–28). Evocations of nature became more and more frequent in manuscripts of this period and expressed a singular desire to show specific aspects of the real world. At this point, landscape began to be an autonomous genre of painting, and was characterized by the appearance of the famous "copses" (*boqueteaux*), a word used in the designation of one of Charles V's chief illuminators. From all these diverse elements emerged a vigorous, earthy style, one already "realistic" in its own way. Its appearance in the Parisian milieu has sometimes been attributed to painters of Flemish or Dutch background who had come to work in the capital. Although the presence of artists from the north was an undeniable stimulant, the new orientation of French painting and illumination seems to have been largely the result of an inner evolution. Besides, how could the new style have imposed itself from without, if it hadn't been congenial to the French artistic milieu within which it flowered, and if it had not been responsive to the aspirations of the Court?

The most typical examples of this style are usually traced back to the reign of Charles V. But this has resulted in the importance of Jean le Bon's patronage being overlooked for far too long. Everything indicates that the new style had already reached its maturity in his time. Several manuscripts executed for the Court around 1350–1355 bear irrefutable witness to this opinion. One of the most important is a *Bible Moralisée* (Paris, Bibliothèque Nationale, Ms. Fr. 167), which is most likely the identifiable Bible mentioned in the royal expense rolls for which Jean le Bon spent considerable amounts from 1349 to 1352. Its 5,212 images painted by some fifteen different artists furnish excellent proof of the various stylistic trends in Parisian illumination during that period, making it safe to assume that its evolution was a continuation as much as a breaking away. Artists of very different styles worked side by side on this Bible. Some remained faithful

XI

to Pucelle's models which they interpreted in a mannerist fashion; others, on the contrary, sought renewal through a direct observation of reality, which they depicted as it appeared to them, without any attempt at embellishment. The two best representations of this "naturalist" trend seem to have come from entirely different artistic backgrounds, although their aesthetic concepts were obviously similar. The figures of the first are vibrant with life, ill-proportioned yet marvelously expressive (Plate 20), which may indicate a Netherlandish background. His collaborator, on the other hand, is more reserved, with a sensitive linear style that aims for exactitude, in keeping with French tradition (Plate 19). The latter's work reappears in two important liturgical manuscripts, a missal for the use of Saint Denis that may be dated around 1350 (Plates 21–22), and a pontifical, executed between 1351 and 1356 for Pierre de Treigny, Bishop of Senlis (Paris, Bibliothèque Sainte-Geneviève, Ms. 148). The artist's contribution to *The Missal of Saint-Denis* is particularly interesting since, in this manuscript, he introduced a new approach to the historiated initial (Plate 22). But the artist's best works can be found in a secular volume of poetry, a copy of the works of Guillaume de Machaut, rather than in these liturgical manuscripts. This volume of poetry is the earliest of the manuscripts that were illustrated during the poet's lifetime. (Paris, Bibliothèque Nationale, Ms. Fr. 1586, Plates 23–26). Philologists have traditionally, though incorrectly, dated this manuscript as 15th century, while art historians have ignored it almost entirely. In actuality, the manuscript goes back to the years 1350–1355, as is proven both by the style of the illuminations and the content of the volume which contains none of Machaut's works after 1350 (even the *Dit du Roi de Navarre* of 1349 is not included).

Our artist illustrated only *Le Remède de Fortune*, the most important work in the volume. The remainder were done by two other illuminators who obviously belong to his school. Machaut's subjects (the celebration of courtly love, and the praise of nature) found their ideal interpreters in these three artists, and especially in the main artist. In this manuscript they were given the opportunity to express their keen sense of observation, for instance in details of dress such as a lady's fashionable outfit, without deviating from truth and nature. More than

XII

his collaborators, the illustrator of *Le Remède de Fortune* shows an ease in the movement of his personages which is unprecedented even in Pucelle's work. They are set in an ambience (interior as well as outdoor scenes) which conveys an authentic impression of space. The illuminations in this manuscript are important on another level as well: they include one of the very first attempts at depicting independent landscape (Plate 26). The style of the illustrator of *Le Remède de Fortune* and of his collaborators was completely novel in Parisian illumination of that period, but seems to have had its antecedents in easel painting whose evolution toward naturalism may have been accelerated in northern France, and especially in Paris, because of a visit the future King Jean le Bon paid in 1342 to the pontifical court in Avignon. His visit coincided with the enlistment by the newly elected Pope Clement VI of a team of painters directed by Matteo Giovanetti of Sienna, who were to decorate the walls of the papal palace. A painting depicting Jean le Bon handing a diptych to Clement VI (Figure IX), bears witness to the impression the Avignon workshop made on the artists who had accompanied the future King of France on this occasion. It was formerly kept in the Sainte-Chapelle and is today known only through a mediocre drawing of Gaignières. The scene was probably painted shortly after the trip to Avignon and seems to be the earliest example of portrait painting in France. The artist already showed great skill in the evocation of space, as well as in painstaking attention to the details of vestments—all points which herald the artist of *Le Remède de Fortune.* A few drawings of that period which are the work of painters and not of illuminators, such as the beautiful courtly scene in a drawing in the Berlin Museum (Figure X), confirm that the style of Machaut's illustrator had its exact counterpart in the easel painting practiced at the Court of France.

The manuscripts which the illustrator of *Le Remède de Fortune* illuminated span a short period of time which seems to indicate that this artist's career may have been even briefer than Pucelle's. He was less fortunate than Pucelle in that he did not have the opportunity to train any disciples on his own level. But the new mood and style which he introduced to Parisian illumination was promptly imitated by a pleiad of artists whose activity corresponded almost exactly to the reign of Charles V. One of the foremost among these followers was the illuminator usually referred to as the *Maître aux Boqueteaux,* because of the small clusters of trees that studded his landscapes, although he neither originated, nor used them exclusively. This artist appeared during the last years of Jean le Bon's effective reign (one of his earliest works, together with *The Bible of Jean de Sy,* is a *Bible Historiale* in the British Library, dated 1357). He seems to have replaced the illustrator of *Le Remède de Fortune* in the King's and the Court's favor. A work which stands out from his abundant but rather monotonous production is his illustration of *The Bible of Jean de Sy;* here, his style is already fully formed, and a number of the unfinished illustrations show his remarkable skill as a draftsman (Figure XI). His most careful, successful works are undeniably the two *grisailles* placed at the beginning of a copy of Guillaume de Machaut, executed toward the end of that great poet's life (Plates 29–30). Despite the obvious talent that is apparent in these two scenes, this illuminator cannot be identified with the painter Jean Bondol, whose only known work is the frontispiece of Jean de Vaudetar's Bible, a *grisaille* which reveals a truly superior artist. At most, one might admit Bondol's influence on the *Maître aux Boqueteaux.*

Another of Charles V's official illuminators is the Master of *The Coronation Book of Charles V*, his best work, which consists of a cycle of illustrations recording the coronation ceremony in 1364, painted shortly after the event (Plates 27–28). This artist was a direct disciple of the illustrator of *Le Remède de Fortune* in whose workshop he must have been formed and with whom he collaborated in the copy of Guillaume de Machaut, Ms. Fr. 1586 in the Bibliothèque Nationale in Paris. His evolution is clearly traceable from the works of his youth to his latest

XIII

productions. At first he imitated his master's style, though rather stiffly, and with dryness, but gradually his design grew more supple. From 1370 on, his meager, sickly personages put on flesh, perhaps under the influence of the *Maître aux Boqueteaux,* whose good-natured roundness he nonetheless never quite assimilated.

A third artist stands out in Charles V's team of book illustrators. His ultimate masterpiece is a *grisaille* depicting the coronation of the young Charles VI, placed at the beginning of Charles V's *Grandes Chroniques de France* (Plate 35). Although done in the same overall style, his works stand out from those of his colleagues thanks to the graceful movement of their personages whose almost feminine faces are drawn in an easy, flawless hand.

Despite their respective talents these different artists—as well as a few others of lesser quality who shared in the royal commissions—never attained the level of their great predecessors, Pucelle and the illustrator of *Le Remède de Fortune.* They rarely repeated the innovations in spatial and scenic treatment which characterized the work of these two artists. At this point, Parisian illumination lived on its past experience, and there was a pause in its creative evolution. The King and his entourage must have been aware of their illustrators' limitations because they occasionally called upon the best painters of the Court to illustrate certain manuscripts. This is especially true of the Bible which the King's advisor, Jean de Vaudetar, offered to Charles V. The King had a remarkable dedication scene, recalling the donation, inserted at the beginning (Plate 36). It was painted in *grisaille* by Jean Bondol of Bruges, who proudly acknowledges it in an inscription in gold letters on the facing page. This splendid piece, done with an extraordinarily subtle brush, reveals all the vigorous realism of the Flemish genius, tempered by a precision and a sobriety in the composition which Bondol probably acquired through contact with his French colleagues.

The astonishing series of images in a manuscript of jurisprudence, the *Hommages du comté de Clermont,* was probably also illustrated by a painter. The manuscript lists the fiefs of this county which belonged to Louis II of Bourbon, Charles V's brother-in-law. Despite the regrettable disappearance of the original, destroyed in 1737 during a fire in the *Chambre des Comptes,* a copy executed shortly before that for Robert de Gaignières allows us to sense the illustrator's feeling for monumental compositions, as well as his excellence as a portrait painter. This is shown in the scene of feudal homage which the Duke of Bourbon was rendering to the King of France, who was depicted surrounded by the principal dignitaries of his Court (Figure XII).

A third manuscript from the end of the period of our study also shows the intervention of a painter. This is the fragment of Jean de Berry's *Très Belles Heures de Notre-Dame* at the Bibliothèque Nationale in Paris (Plate 40). The aesthetic purpose of the manuscript is clear and it corresponds so perfectly to the Duke's taste for experimentation which can be seen in several of his later manuscripts. The illustrations of the *Très Belles Heures* reveal a feeling of volume and space that was alien to the illuminators at that time, and are definitely the work of a painter. He is readily recognizable as the author of the *Parement de Narbonne* and was, next to Jean Bondol, the best artist of Charles V's time. His unusual tonalities and careful blendings show the gifts, as a painter, of this artist whose masterpiece at the Louvre is done in *grisaille* (Figure XIII). His work has lost nothing of its monumental strength in the transfer to parchment. Still solidly anchored, by his style, in 14th-century tradition, his illustrations already manifested the formal refinements which French illumination was next to develop at the instigation of Jean de Berry. There is something fatidical about the history of this manuscript. Left unfinished by the Master of the *Parement de Narbonne,* it was later given, first to the Limbourgs, and then to Jan van Eyck to complete.

SELECTED BIBLIOGRAPHY

General

F. Baron, "*Enlumineurs, peintres et sculpteurs parisiens du 14ème et 15ème siècles d'après les Archives de l'Hôpital Saint-Jacques*," in the *Bulletin archéologique du Comité des travaux historiques et scientifiques* (1970) 1971, 77–115.

L. Delisle, *Recherches sur la librairie de Charles V*. Paris 1907, 2 vols.

P. Durrieu, "*La peinture en France de Jean le Bon à Charles V (1350–1380)*," in *Histoire de l'Art* by André Michel, vol. III, first part. Paris 1907, pp. 101–137.

H. Martin, *La miniature française du XIIIe au XVe siècle*. Paris, Brussels 1923.

M. Meiss, *French Painting in the Time of Jean de Berry*, I. *The Late 14th century and the Patronage of the Duke*. London 1967, 2 vols.

K. Morand, *Jean Pucelle*. Oxford 1962.

C. Nordenfalk, "Maître Honoré and Maître Pucelle," *Apollo* LXXIX (1964), 358–364.

E. Panofsky, *Early Netherlandish Painting, its Origins and Character*. Cambridge, (Mass.) 1953, 2 vols.

J. Porcher, *L'Enluminure française*. Paris 1959.

C. R. Sherman, *The Portraits of Charles V of France (1338–1380)*. New York 1969.

G. Schmidt, review of: C. R. Sherman, *The Portraits of Charles V of France*, in *Zeitschrift fur Kunstgeschichte* (1971), 72–88.

C. Sterling [Jacques], *La peinture française. Les peintres du Moyen Age*. Paris 1941.

G. Vitzthum, *Die Pariser Miniaturmalerei von der Zeit des hl. Ludwig bis zu Philipp von Valois*. Leipzig 1907.

J. White, *The Birth and Rebirth of Pictorial Space*. London 1967. (Chapter XIV: *Fourteenth and Fifteenth-Century Manuscript Illumination in France*.)

Exhibitions

Les Manuscrits à peinture en France du XIIIe au XVIe siècle, Paris, Bibliothèque Nationale, 1955.

La Librairie de Charles V, Paris, Bibliothèque Nationale, 1968.

L'Art et la Cour. France et Angleterre 1259–1328, Ottawa, Galerie Nationale du Canada, 1972.

Bibliography to Individual Manuscripts.

Plate 1:

H. Martin, *Légende de Saint Denis. Reproduction des miniatures du manuscrit original présenté en 1317 au Roi Philippe le Long*. Paris 1908.

C. Lacaze, Parisius-Paradisus, "An aspect of the Vie de St. Denis Manuscript of 1317," *Marsyas* XVI (1972–1973), 60–66.

V. W. Egbert, *On the Bridges of Medieval Paris. A Record of Early Fourteenth-Century Life*. Princeton 1974.

Plate 2:

V. Leroquais, *Les Sacramentaires et les missels manuscrits des bibliothèques publiques de France*, Tome II. Paris 1924, pp. 248–249.

Plates 3–10:

L. Delisle, *Les Heures dites de Jean Pucelle, manuscrit de la collection de M. le Baron Maurice de Rothschild*. Paris 1910.

J. J. Rorimer, *The Hours of Jeanne d'Évreux, Queen of France*. New York 1957.

K. Morand, *Jean Pucelle*. Oxford 1962, pp. 13–16, 41–42.

J. Hoffeld, "An Image of St. Louis and the Structuring of Devotion," *Bulletin of the Metropolitan Museum of Art* XXIX (1971), 261–266.

L. J. Randall, "Games and the Passion in Pucelle's *Hours of Jeanne d'Évreux*," *Speculum* XLVII (1972), 246–257.

Plates 11–12:

V. Leroquais, *Les Bréviaires manuscrits des bibliothèques publiques de France*, Tome III. Paris 1934, pp. 198–210.

F. G. Godwin, "An Illustration to the *De Sacramentis* of St. Thomas Aquinas," *Speculum* XXVI (1951), 609–614.

K. Morand, *op. cit.*, pp. 9–12, 43–45.

Plate 13:

H. Focillon, *Le Peintre des Miracles de Notre-Dame*. Paris 1950.

K. Morand, *op cit.*, pp. 42–43.

Plate 14:

G. Gagnebin, *"Une Bible Historiale de l'atelier de Jean Pucelle,"* in *Genava* n.s. IV (1956), 23–65.

K. Morand, *op. cit.*, pp. 8–9, 40.

Plate 15:

H. Yates Thompson, *Thirty-two Miniatures from the Book of Hours of Joan III, Queen of Navarre.* London 1899.

M. R. James, *A Descriptive Catalogue of the second Series of fifty Mss. in the Collection of Henry Yates Thompson.* London 1902, pp. 151–183 (entry by S. C. Cockerell).

K. Morand, *op. cit.*, pp. 20–21, 48–49.

F. Avril, *"Trois manuscrits de l'entourage de Jean Pucelle,"* in *Revue de l'Art* No. 9 (1970), 45, 48.

M. Thomas, *"L'Iconographie de Saint Louis dans les Heures de Jeanne de Navarre,"* in *Septième Centenaire de la mort de Saint Louis, Actes des colloques de Royaumont et de Paris* (May 21–27, 1970), Paris 1976, 209–231.

Plate 18:

K. Morand, *op. cit.*, pp. 21–22, 40.

F. Deuchler, "Looking at Bonne of Luxembourg's Prayer Book," *Bulletin of the Metropolitan Museum* XXIX (1971), 268–278.

C. Vaurie, "Birds in the Prayer Book of Bonne of Luxembourg," *ibid.*, 279–281.

Plates 19–20:

P. Durrieu, *"Manuscrits de luxe exécutés pour des princes et grands seigneurs français,"* in *Le Manuscrit* II (1895), 103, 114–118.

A. de Laborde, *Étude sur la Bible moralisée illustrée,* Tome V. Paris 1927, pp. 92–102, plates 724–738.

F. Avril, *"Un chef-d'oeuvre de l'enluminure sous le règne de Jean le Bon, la Bible moralisée, manuscrit français de la Bibliothèque Nationale,"* in *Monuments et mémoires de la Fondation Eugène Piot* 58 (1972), 95–125.

G. Schmidt, *"Zur Datiuring des 'Kleinen' Bargello-Diptychons und der Verkundigungstafel* in Cleveland," in *Études d'art offertes à Charles Sterling.* Paris 1975, p. 57.

Plates 21–22:

A. Wilmart, *"Les Anniversaires célébrés à Saint-Denis au milieu du XIVe siècle,"* in *Revue Mabillon* XIV (1924), 22–31.

F. Avril, *art. cit.*, pp. 112–114.

G. Schmidt, *loc. cit.*

Plates 23–26:

E. Hoepffner, ed.: *Oeuvres de Guillaume de Machaut.* Paris 1908–1921, 3 vols. *(Société des anciens textes français).*

U. Günther, *"Chronologie und Stil der Kompositionen Guillaume de Machauts,"* in *Acta Musicologica* XXX (1963), 96–114.

S. S. Williams, "An Author's role in Fourteenth-Century Book Production: Guillaume de Machaut's *'livre ou je mets toutes mes choses',"* in *Romania* 90 (1969), 433–454.

F. Avril, *art. cit.*, pp. 112–114.

G. Schmidt, *loc. cit.*

Plates 27–28:

E. S. Dewick, *The Coronation Book of Charles V of France (Cottonian Ms. Tiberius B. VIII).* London 1899 (Henry Bradshaw Society, Vol. XVI).

L. Delisle, *Recherches sur la librairie de Charles V,* Tome I. Paris 1907, pp. 218–219.

C. R. Sherman, *The Portraits of Charles V of France.* New York 1969, pp. 34–37.

Plates 29–30:

E. Hoepffner, *op. cit.*

H. Martin, *La Miniature française du XIIIe au XVe siècle.* Paris 1923, pls. LXV–LXVI.

Plate 31:

L. Delisle, *op. cit.*, Tome I, pp. 320–321.

M. Lièvre, *"Note sur le manuscrit original du Songe du Verger et sur la librairie de Charles V,"* in *Romania* 77 (1956), 352–360.

Plate 32:

L. Delisle, *op. cit.*, Tome I, pp. 283–284.

A. Boinet, *"Les manuscrits à peintures de la Bibliothèque Sainte-Geneviève de Paris,"* in *Bulletin de la Société française de reproduction de manuscrits à peintures* V (1921), 86–96.

D. Hillard, *Le Tite Live de Charles V, manuscrit de la Bibliothèque Sainte-Geneviève.* Paris 1969.

Plate 33:

L. Delisle, *op. cit.*, Tome I, pp. 104–107, 254–255.

G. Gaspar and F. Lyna, *Les principaux manuscrits à peintures de la Bibliothèque Royale de Bruxelles,* (First Part). Paris 1937, pp. 254-356.

L. M. J. Delaissé, *Miniatures médiévales dans la librairie de Bourgogne au Cabinet des Manuscrits de la Bibliothèque Royale de Belgique.* Brussels 1959, pp. 78–81.

C. R. Sherman, *The Portraits of Charles V of France.* New York 1969, pp. 28–30.

Plates 34–35:

L. Delisle, *op. cit.*, Tome I, pp. 312–314.

R. Delachenal, *Chronique des règnes de Jean II et de Charles V.* Paris 1920 *(Société de l'histoire de France).*

M. Thomas, *"La Visite de l'Empereur Charles IV en France, d'après l'exemplaire des 'Grandes Chroniques' exécuté pour le Roi Charles V,"* in *VIe Congrès international des Bibliophiles, Vienna, September 29 to October 5, 1969* (Vienna 1971), 85–89.

Plate 36:

L. Delisle, *op. cit.*, Tome I, pp. 148–149.

A. W. Byvanck, *Les Principaux manuscrits à peintures de la Bibliothèque Royale des Pays-Bas et du Musée Meermanno-Westreenianum à la Haye.* Paris 1924, pp. 104–110.

E. Panofsky, *Early Netherlandish Painting.* Cambridge (Mass.) 1953, pp. 35–36.

M. Meiss, *French Painting in the Time of Jean de Berry. The Late XIVth century.* London 1967, pp. 21–22.

C. R. Sherman, *op. cit.*, pp. 26–28.

Plate 37:

L. Delisle, *op. cit.*, Tome I, pp. 187–190.

V. Leroquais, *Les Bréviaires manuscrits des bibliothèques publiques de France,* Tome III. Paris 1934, pp. 49ff.

K. Morand, *op. cit.*, pp. 25–28.

M. Meiss, *op. cit.*, pp. 160–161.

C. R. Sherman, *op. cit.*, pp. 47–48.

Plate 38:

L. Delisle, *op. cit.*, Tome I, pp. 152–153.

K. Morand, *op. cit.*, p. 42.

F. Avril, "*Une Bible Historiale de Charles V,*" in *Jahrbuch der Hamburger Kunstsammlungen* 14–15 (1970), 45–76.

Plate 39:

V. Leroquais, *Les Livres d'heures manuscrits de la Bibliothèque Nationale,* Tome II. Paris 1927, pp. 175–187.

K. Morand, *op. cit.*, pp. 26–27.

L. M. J. Delaissé, "*Remaniements dans quelques manuscrits de Jean de Berry,*" in *Essais en l'honneur de Jean Porcher,* ed. O. Pächt. Paris 1963, pp. 129–133.

M. Meiss, *op. cit.*, pp. 160–169.

Plate 40:

P. Durrieu, *Les Très Belles Heures de Notre-Dame du duc Jean de Berry.* Paris, 1922.

L. M. J. Delaissé, *art. cit.*, pp. 133–139.

M. Meiss, *op. cit.*, pp. 99–134, 337–340.

E. S. Spencer "The first Patron on the *Très Belles Heures de Notre-Dame,*" in *Scriptorium,* XXIII (1969), 145–149.

Bibliography of Black-and-White Figures

Figure I

P. Aubry, *Le Roman de Fauvel, Reproduction photographique du manuscrit francais 146 de la Bibliothèque Nationale de Paris,* 1907.

Figure II

G. Vitzthum, *Die Pariser Miniaturmalerei*, pp. 78–83.

P. Durrieu, "*Un siècle de l'histoire de l'enluminure parisienne à partir du règne de Saint Louis,*" in *Journal des savants* (1909), 16–17.

R. Freyhan, "*Ein englischer Buchmaler in Paris zu Beginn des 14. Jahrhunderts,*" in *Marburger Jahrbuch für Kunstwissenschaft* VI (1931), 1–9.

Figure III

L. Delisle, "*La Bible de Robert de Billyng et de Jean Pucelle,*" in *Revue de l'art chrétien* (1910), 297–308.

K. Morand, *op. cit.*, pp. 5–6, 47–48.

Figure IV

L. Delisle, *art. cit.*

K. Morand, *op. cit.*, pp. 45–47.

Figures V–VI

H. Focillon, *Le peintre des Miracles de Notre-Dame.* Paris 1950.

K. Morand, *op. cit.*, pp. 42–43.

Figure VII

J. Taralon, *Les Trésors des églises de France.* Paris 1966, pp. 143–145.

M. Meiss, *op. cit.*, p. 100.

Figure VIII

S. C. Cockerell, *The Book of Hours of Yolande of Flanders.* London 1905.

K. Morand, *op. cit.*, pp. 22–23, 41.

M. Meiss, *op. cit.*, pp. 167–168.

Figure IX

O. Pächt, "The Avignon Diptych and its Eastern Ancestry," in *De artibus opuscula, Essays in honor of E. Panofsky,* ed. M. Meiss. New York 1961, pp. 402–421.

M. Kahr, "Jean le Bon in Avignon," *Paragone* (1966), 3–16.

Figure XI

L. Delisle, *Recherches sur la librairie de Charles V,* Tome I, pp. 146, 328–330.

H. Martin, *La Miniature française*, pp. 37–44.

M. Meiss, *op. cit.*, pp. 20, 141, 152, 315.

Figure XII

C. R. Sherman, *op. cit.*, pp. 40–41.

Figure XIII

C. Sterling, H. Adhémar, N. Reynaud, *Musée National du Louvre, Peinture. Ecole française, XIVe, XVe, and XVIe siècles.* Paris 1965, pp. 1–2, pls. 2–7.

M. Meiss, *op. cit.*, pp. 99–107, 113–118, 130–133, figs. 1–5.

LIST OF COLOR PLATES AND BLACK-AND-WHITE FIGURES

I. THE LIFE OF SAINT DENIS
Paris, Bibliothèque Nationale, Ms. Fr. 2090–2092
240 x 160 mm

The manuscript of *The Life of Saint Denis* was begun during the reign of Philip IV (The Fair) at the urging of Jean de Pontoise, Abbot of Saint Denis, but was not completed until 1317, when it was presented to Philip V (The Tall). At this time, the manuscript consists of three volumes (Bibl. Nat., French 2090–2092), and an additional fragment which must have been separated from the complete work at an earlier period (Bibl. Nat., Latin 13836). There are seventy-seven paintings altogether, depicting the life and martyrdom of Saint Denis, first Bishop of Paris, whom his initial hagiographers regrettably confused with the Athenian saint Denys the Areopagite. Despite its exceptional richness, the work represents only a fraction of the complete cycle, a reflection of which has been preserved in a contemporary copy illustrated with pen and ink drawings (Bibl. Nat., Latin 5286).

Plate 1. *Saint Denis, Saint Saintin and Saint Antonin,* Ms. Fr. 2091 (Vol. II), fol. 125

II. MISSAL FOR THE USE OF PARIS
Paris, Bibliothèque Nationale, Ms. Lat. 861
300 x 210 mm

Nothing is known about the history of this Missal prior to the 15th century, when it belonged to the Confraternity of Notre-Dame of the burghers of Paris. However, the extreme care taken in its execution, as well as the quality of its ornamentation, lead us to believe that it was initially destined for some royal chapel; an assumption further confirmed by the presence of the Arms of France alternating with the Arms of Navarre which checker the background of the painting on fol. 148. They can only refer to one of the three sons of Philip The Fair: Louis X (The Quarrelsome), Philip V (The Tall), or Charles IX (The Fair), the only Kings of France of the Capetian branch to have been titular Kings of Navarre. In that case, the volume would have had to have been produced between 1314 and 1328, as the style also indicates.

Plate 2. *The Crucifixion,* fol. 147v

III. THE HOURS OF JEANNE D'ÉVREUX
New York, The Cloisters Museum of The Metropolitan Museum of Art
94 x 64 mm

The identification of this precious little manuscript with "the very small pocket prayerbook" which King Charles IV (The Fair) of France gave to his wife Jeanne d'Évreux need no longer be questioned. It is undeniably Jean Pucelle's masterpiece, as well as one of the most original creations in 14th-century French illumination. In 1371 Jeanne d'Évreux bequeathed it to Charles V; it later reappeared in the collection of Jean de Berry who had several of the grotesque figures copied for his *Grandes Heures.*

Plate 3. *The Arrest of Christ on Mount Olivet* and *The Annunciation,* fol. 15v–fol. 16
Plate 4. *Christ before Pontius Pilate* and *The Visitation,* fol. 34v–fol. 35
Plate 5. *Christ Carrying the Cross* and *The Annunciation to the Shepherds,* fol. 61v–fol. 62
Plate 6. *The Crucifixion* and *The Adoration of the Magi,* fol. 68v–fol. 69
Plate 7. *The Lamentation over the Body of Christ* and *The Flight into Egypt,* fol. 82v–fol. 83
Plate 8. *Queen Jeanne d'Évreux at the Tomb of Saint Louis* and *The Education of Saint Louis,* fol. 102v–fol. 103
Plate 9. *Saint Louis: The Miraculous Return of his Breviary* and *Decorated Text Page,* fol. 154v–fol. 155
Plate 10. *Saint Louis Burying the Bones of the Crusaders* and *Decorated Text Page,* fol. 159v–fol. 160

IV. THE BELLEVILLE BREVIARY
Paris, Bibliothèque Nationale, Ms. Lat. 10483–10484
240 x 170 mm

The Belleville Breviary, which appears under that designation in Charles V's inventories, seems to have derived its name from its probable recipient, Jeanne de Belleville, the wife of Olivier de Clisson, whose belongings were confiscated by the Crown in 1343. Charles VI gave the manuscript as a gift to his son-in-law Richard II of England, but it soon came back across the Channel when Richard II's successor Henry IV donated it to the Duke de Berry, probably at the latter's request. Its Dominican use explains, no doubt, the fact that the Duke agreed to turn it over to his niece Marie de France, a nun in the convent at Poissy, where the manuscript remained until the Revolution.

Plate 11. *December,* Ms. Lat. 10483 (Tome I), fol. 6v
Plate 12. *Confirmation,* Ms. Lat. 10483 (Tome I), fol. 37

V. THE MIRACLES OF OUR LADY
Paris, Bibliothèque Nationale, Ms. Nouv. Acq. Fr. 24541
340 x 242 mm

This luxurious copy of *The Miracles of Our Lady,* composed at the beginning of the 13th century by Gauthier de Coincy, Prior of Vic-sur-Aisne, seems to have been intended for Jeanne de Bourgogne, the wife of Philip VI of Valois. She is probably the queen who is shown in prayer before the Virgin on several of the painted miniatures at the end of the volume. The manuscript was seized by the English in the personal effects of John the Good during the battle of Poitiers (1356); Charles V bought it back and it passed into the collections of his brother, Jean de Berry, who was an ardent admirer of Pucelle's work.

Plate 13A. *The Abduction of the Little Nun,* fol. 93
Plate 13B. *The Laborer and his Plow,* fol. 172

VI. THE GENEVA BIBLE HISTORIALE
Geneva, Bibliothèque Publique et Universitaire, Ms. Fr. 2
385 x 297 mm

Plate 14. *Christ in Majesty,* fol. 1

VII. THE HOURS OF JEANNE DE NAVARRE
Paris, Bibliothèque Nationale, Ms. Nouv. Acq. Lat. 3145
178 x 135 mm

It was Sir Sidney Cockerell who discovered that this luxurious Book of Hours belonged to Jeanne de Navarre (1311–1349), daughter of Louis X (The Quarrelsome), King of France. Her name is mentioned in one of the final prayers and her Coat of Arms, as well as those of her husband, Philip d'Évreux, appear on many pages. It is more difficult to determine the date of the manuscript, which must be placed after the year 1329, when Jeanne was crowned Queen of Navarre. Since the Arms of Champagne do not appear in the manuscript, and since Jeanne had renounced this appanage in favor of the King of France in 1336, Cockerell placed the execution of the paintings after this date. Later, Marcel Thomas proposed a series of arguments based on his study of the cycle of illustrations in the Hours of Saint Louis in the manuscript that would place the date between 1333 and 1334. Various stylistic considerations seem to speak in favor of placing the date after 1336.

Plate 15. *The Annunciation to the Shepherds,* fol. 53
Plate 16. *The Adoration of the Magi,* fol. 55v
Plate 17. *The Arrest of Christ on Mount Olivet,* fol. 109

VII. THE PSALTER OF BONNE DE LUXEMBOURG
New York, The Cloisters Museum of The Metropolitan Museum of Art
126 x 88 mm

The Arms which are repeated at the bottom of the paintings identify the owner of this manuscript as Bonne of Luxembourg. Bonne was educated at the court of France which her father, John of Luxembourg, King of Bohemia, often visited. In 1332 she married John of Normandy and died in September 1349, only a few months before her husband acceded to the throne of France as King John II. The paintings in this Psalter, all in *grisaille,* probably go back to the end of Bonne's life. At one point they were attributed to Pucelle, but from a stylistic point of view they are related to the works of Jean Le Noir, although they lack the latter's dramatic violence and virulent caricature. The almost feminine smoothness of the design and certain weaknesses of the composition (as, for instance, in *The Arrest of Christ*) suggest that the execution may have been done, at least in part, by Jean Le Noir's foremost collaborator, his very own daughter, Bourgot, who is known to have been an illuminator and to have worked with her father.

Plate 18A. *Psalm 52* and *Decorated Text Page,* fol. 83v–fol. 84
Plate 18B. *The Three Living* and *The Three Dead,* fol. 321v–fol. 322

IX. THE BIBLE MORALISÉE OF JEAN LE BON
Paris, Bibliothèque Nationale, Ms. Fr. 167
410 x 290 mm

The *Bible Moralisée* is a form of illustrated biblical exegesis, first conceived by religious scholars in the service of the royal family of France, and for the use of the latter, during the first half of the 13th century. Bible passages alternate with their "moralized" interpretation, each accompanied by illustrations in an opposing column. There are two columns of illustrations, with four images per column. Dated for a long time at the end of the 14th century, this copy was most likely commissioned by King Jean le Bon at the beginning of his reign.

Plate 19. *The Life of Saint Paul,* fol. 285v
Plate 20. *Samson and Delilah,* fol. 59

X. THE MISSAL OF SAINT-DENIS
London, Victoria and Albert Museum, Ms. 1346–1891.
233 x 164 mm

Judging by its liturgical use, this luxurious Missal was made for the Abbey of Saint-Denis. In view of the relationship which existed between the Abbey and the French monarchy (since the 13th century at least, the Abbey was used as a royal necropolis and the emblems used during the Coronation ceremonies were kept there), it may be assumed that the manuscript was offered to the Abbey by a member of the royal family. The various obits of Kings of France and Abbots of Saint-Denis which appear in the calendar establish the execution date of the volume as around 1350–1351.

Plate 21. *The Miracle of the Leprous Pilgrim,* fol. 256v
Plate 22. *Saint Denis Aids Dagobert,* fol. 261

XI. GUILLAUME DE MACHAUT: LE RÈMEDE DE FORTUNE, LE DIT DU LION
Paris, Bibliothèque Nationale, Ms. Fr. 1586
300 x 210 mm

Plate 23. *The Lover Contemplates his Lady,* fol. 23
Plate 24. *The Lover Sings as his Lady Dances,* fol. 51
Plate 25. *The Banquet,* fol. 55
Plate 26. *The Enchanted Garden,* fol. 103

XII. THE CORONATION BOOK OF CHARLES V
London, The British Library, Cotton Tiberius B. VIII
280 x 190 mm

Plate 27. *King Charles in the Palace of the Archbishop of Reims,* fol. 44v
Plate 28. *King Charles Receives the Kiss of his Peers,* fol. 64

XIII. GUILLAUME DE MACHAUT, POETIC WORKS
Paris, Bibliothèque Nationale, Ms. Fr. 1586
300 x 210 mm

This manuscript, which contains the complete literary works of Guillaume de Machaut, including his historical poem *La Prise d'Alexandrie* (composed around 1370–1371), was probably executed and illustrated while the poet was still alive (he died in 1377). The recipient of the volume is not known. Annotations in English on the last double page indicate that it must have had an English owner before Louis de la Gruthuyse, a gentleman from Bruges, and a great lover of books, bought it for his collection toward the end of the 15th century. The latter's Coat of Arms on Folio D was covered over by the Coat of Arms of France when King Louis XII acquired de la Gruthuyse's manuscripts (Plate 30). The slightly raised pen and ink illustrations within the text are by an artist who is known for this work alone. Although this volume shows a strong stylistic kinship with other illuminated manuscripts executed for the Court, it may have been illustrated in Reims (Machaut was Canon of the cathedral) by a local illuminator who worked under the poet's direction. The two preliminary *grisailles* are additions made in Paris by the *Maître aux Boqueteaux.*

Plate 29. *Nature Introduces her Children to the Poet,* fol. E
Plate 30. *Love Introduces his Children to the Poet,* fol. D

XIV. LE SONGE DU VERGER
London, The British Library, Ms. Royal 19 C. IV.
315 x 240 mm

Plate 31. *The Churchman and the Knight Debate,* fol. 1v

XV. THE LIVY OF CHARLES V
Paris, Bibliothèque Sainte-Geneviève, Ms. 777
455 x 310 mm

Plate 32. *Roman History,* fol. 7

XVI. ARISTOTLE'S ETHICS
Brussels, Bibliothèque Royale, Ms. 9505–6
320 x 215 mm

Plate 33. *Dedication Scene; The King and his Family; Two Scenes of Instruction,* fol. 2v

XVII. CHARLES V'S GRANDES CHRONIQUES DE FRANCE
Paris, Bibliothèque Nationale, Ms. Fr. 2813
330 x 220 mm

Plate 34. *The Reception for Emperor Charles IV,* fol. 473v
Plate 35. *The Coronation of Charles VI,* fol. 3v

XVIII. THE BIBLE HISTORIALE OF JEAN DE VAUDETAR
The Hague, Musee Meermanno-Westreenianum, Ms. 10 B. 23
295 x 215 mm

Plate 36. *Presentation to the King,* fol. 2

XIX. THE BREVIARY OF CHARLES V
Bibliothèque Nationale, Ms. Lat. 1052
230 x 178 mm

Plate 37. *Psalm 109,* fol. 261

XX. THE BIBLE HISTORIALE OF CHARLES V
Paris, Bibliothèque de l'Arsenal, Ms. 5212
283 x 192 mm

Charles V was a fervent student of the Bible, which he made a point of honor of reading from cover to cover each year, as Christine de Pisan informs us. The library of Charles V contained a great number of copies of the French adaptation of the Bible which was very popular at the time: The *Bible Historiale* by Guyart des Moulins (Plate 14). The most remarkable example of this text from the royal collections is decidedly the copy which the Bibliothèque de l'Arsenal and the Kunsthalle in Hamburg share between them today. Although the two manuscripts were done at the same time, they differ in their execution: the volume in the Arsenal contains paintings in *grisaille,* while the illustrations in the complementary part have been done in color. One other thing distinguishes this royal copy: each volume is introduced by a complex illustration which visually evokes the various Biblical books contained therein. An explanatory text which has been preserved in the Hamburg volume but was lost from the one in the Arsenal, facilitated the interpretations of these unique compositions, which are typical of the 14th-century predilection for sophisticated iconographic programs.

Plate 38. *The Pentateuch; The Historical Books; The Hagiographa; The Prophets,* fol. 1

XXI. THE PETITES HEURES OF JEAN DE BERRY

Paris, Bibliothèque Nationale, Ms. Lat. 18014
215 x 145 mm

The last illuminations painted by Jean Le Noir appear in *The Petites Heures of Jean de Berry.* The manuscript is usually dated around the 1380s, and is assumed to have been executed in a single effort by a team of artists under the direction of Jacquemart de Hesdin, and in collaboration with Jean Le Noir. Actually, two phases can be distinguished in the execution of the volume. The manuscript was probably begun around 1372–1375, at a time when Jean Le Noir appeared in Jean de Berry's accounts, and was left unfinished at the death of the artist, who must have been quite old at the time. It must have been only at a later period that the Duke de Berry recruited Jacquemart de Hesdin and his team to finish the decoration of this Book of Hours. The cycle of the Passion, a painting which introduces the Psalms of Penitence, and one of the scenes from the Office of Saint John the Baptist are the only illustrations entirely done by Le Noir. However, Le Noir must have done a great deal of preparatory work on the other paintings, because a large number of them still clearly bear the mark of his style and of his plans of composition, even though they were later completed by Jacquemart and his collaborators. This is particularly evident in the illustrations of the Offices of the Virgin and of Saint John the Baptist.

Plate 39. *The Arrest of Christ,* fol. 76

XXII. THE TRÈS BELLES HEURES OF JEAN DE BERRY *(Paris Fragment)*

Paris, Bibliothèque Nationale, Ms. Nouv. Acq. Lat. 3093
280 x 200 mm

The extraordinary fate of this famous Book of Hours was authoritatively traced by Count Paul Durrieu at the beginning of this century. Its illustration was begun around 1380, but it was still unfinished shortly before 1413, when the Duke de Berry made a present of the volume to his adviser Robinet d'Etampes. The latter kept only the finished part of the Book of Hours, the fragment which today belongs to the Bibliothèque Nationale in Paris. The remainder reappeared some ten years later at the Dutch Court where Jan van Eyck and various collaborators completed its illustration, probably for Countess Jacqueline of Bavaria. Only one-half of this separate part is still in existence, at the Museo Civico in Turin. The other part disappeared in 1904 when a fire broke out at the Biblioteca Nazionale in Turin.

Plate 40. *Caiaphas Interrogates Christ,* p. 189

Black-and-White Figures

PLATES AND COMMENTARIES

PLATE 1

The Life Of Saint Denis

Vol. II, fol. 125 *Saint Denis, Saint Saintin, and Saint Antonin*

Plate 1 shows Saint Denis urging Saint Saintin and Saint Antonin to write the story of his life. A gilded architectural structure, probably inspired by goldsmithery, gives the scene its frame. The scene itself is divided into two distinct sections: at the top, the Bishop of Paris is seated on an X-shaped throne within a schematically drawn church, addressing his two disciples, while two other members of the clergy stand behind him. An inscription under Saint Denis's feet indicates that the event takes place in Paris.

In the lower half of the painting, the artist revives various aspects of daily life in 14th-century Paris: on the left, a coach filled with travellers enters by one of the city gates. On the right, a doctor examines a urine specimen while taking money from his patient. On the river, three boats loaded with wine barrels glide alongside a quay. In one of them, the boatman is concluding the sale of part of his cargo with a buyer. Another customer is seated in the boat next to it, tasting the wine to check its quality prior to making a purchase. Twenty-nine other miniatures in the manuscript depict various activities of artisans and merchants in the capital; according to a recent theory, they may have been intended as a kind of homage to the "good government" which Paris enjoyed under the Capetian dynasty.

The work of an original personality, these strongly drawn figures, together with the powerful plasticity of the drapery, represent a departure from the exquisite refinement and studied elegance of Honoré and his followers. But, in keeping with tradition, the concept of space still lacks depth perception, despite the stacking of the various scene levels in successive "degrees."

S. anto
S. sanct
S. dyon
parisius
Istos prelatos ad se pater iste uocatos
admonet ut presto sint hy certamine gesto.
Pape gestor seriem defert

PLATE 2

MISSAL FOR THE USE OF PARIS

fol. 147v *The Crucifixion*

The ornamentation of this manuscript consists of a series of historiated initials illustrating the main feasts, and two full-page paintings in the Canon of the Mass—the work of a direct follower of Maître Honoré, the great Parisian illuminator of the end of the 13th century, whose persistent influence can be traced in manuscripts of the capital until approximately the 1330s.

The two paintings in the Canon, which face each other, represent *The Crucifixion* (f. 147v), and *Christ in Majesty* (f. 148), surrounded by the symbols of the Evangelists. *The Crucifixion* is placed inside an elongated three-colored quatrefoil which is, itself, encased in a rectangular frame decorated with gilded leaves; the scene has been reduced to its three principal protagonists, according to traditional iconography: Christ, the Virgin, and Saint John. The two small half-figures on either side of the crucified Christ, representing respectively, The Church and The Synagogue, illustrate the idea that Christ's sacrifice marked, for humanity, the passage from the era *sub lege* (Law) to the era *sub gratia* (Grace).

The crucifixion scene is repeated in the bottom margin on a smaller scale; this was done for an essentially practical purpose: to protect the principal scene from the ritual kisses of the officiating priest. In this instance, the linear lyricism of Honoré and his school is expressed by the pathetic, that is, somewhat mannered, poses of the personages. The extremely plastic treatment of the bodies should also be noted. They stand out from the background like *mezzo-relievo* sculptures giving a tactile impression which is characteristic of the preoccupations with depth which began to appear in French illumination toward the end of the 13th century.

PLATE 3

The Hours of Jeanne D'Évreux

fols. 15v–16 *The Arrest of Christ on Mount Olivet* and *The Annunciation*

In this manuscript, unquestionably the masterpiece of Jean Pucelle, one noteworthy detail stands out in the iconographic plan of the Office of the Virgin: the Childhood scenes which are traditionally represented at the head of each of the canonical hours are here juxtaposed to scenes from the Passion. Pucelle has introduced subtle, discreet resonances between the two series of images.

The cycle begins with *The Annunciation* (f. 16) in Matins, opposite the scene of *The Arrest of Christ on Mount Olivet* (f. 15v). The Virgin, standing inside a small house, is draped in an ample cloak, and haloed in red, hailed by Gabriel who is seen kneeling in the vestibule. Cherubs are watching the scene from the upper windows. In this image, most probably inspired by Duccio, as is the case with other illustrations of the Hours of the Virgin, Pucelle introduces the first spatially coherent representation of an interior to appear in northern Europe. Below, the artist uses the initial *D* of the text as a frame for the devotions of Jeanne d'Évreux: The queen is shown kneeling on a *prie-dieu,* reading her Book of Hours. A guard armed with a club is standing watch outside the door, which has been fitted into the vertical stroke of the letter. In the lower margin, a delightful image shows a group of young people engaged in a game which seems to be a mixture of tag and blindman's bluff.

The concept of *The Arrest of Christ* shown on the facing page differs considerably from *The Annunciation:* The rhythmic alternation of full space with empty space in *The Annunciation* has been replaced by a compact density. Bristling with menacing weapons, the troop of soldiers under Judas's lead forms a hostile milling block which contrasts strikingly with the peaceful group of Christ's disciples. Only Saint Peter makes a belligerent gesture toward Malchus, whose ear Christ is about to heal. The treatment of the grays, and the admirable plasticity of the figures, gives this scene the appearance of carved ivory.

PLATE 4

The Hours of Jeanne D'Évreux

fols. 34v–35 *Christ Before Pontius Pilate* and *The Visitation*

On f. 35, Lauds begins with the usual *Visitation* scene. Mary and Elizabeth meet again, like two old friends after a long separation. They embrace and contemplate each other with dignified reserve. Elizabeth points a questioning index finger at the Virgin. The two women stand out against a background of blue, gaily animated with birds and foliage which the artist has treated in the same *grisaille* technique as the two principal figures. A capital letter formed by thick spirals contains a hybrid being armed with a sword and a shield. In the margin below, two peasants dance a ludicrous dance to the sounds of instruments from an improvised orchestra: a bagpipe player and a fool who is using a cauldron as a drum.

The animals which accompany the main scene have, no doubt, symbolic meaning: the rabbit at the base of *The Visitation* is an allusion to fecundity. The monkey hidden in the upper spiral of the capital letter was said to signify the fall of man, and contemplates the dramatic scene on the facing page (f. 34v), which represents Christ standing before Pontius Pilate. The Roman prefect is shown in profile, seated on a throne, interrogating Christ, who is escorted by Jews and soldiers with strongly drawn features. A young man is bringing Pontius Pilate a pitcher and a towel by which the prefect was conveying to the Jews that the responsibility for Christ's fate was theirs. Two hybrid creatures support the scene while, at the same time, prolonging the parodical feast on the opposite page: the first hybrid is using a dog as a bagpipe, the second is furiously blowing into a horn.

The harmonious cadence of the drapery gives the two scenes their unity. Like most of the scenes which follow, they are encased in a delicate architectural frame with finely chiseled detail which recalls the goldsmithery of the time. Drawn like architectural projects, the frames give rise to the notion that Pucelle, who is known to have designed the seal of the Confraternity of Saint-Jacques-aux-Pélerins, may also have supplied "models" for shrines and reliquaries.

3

4

PLATE 5

THE HOURS OF JEANNE D'ÉVREUX

fols. 61v–62 *Christ Carrying the Cross* and *The Annunciation to the Shepherds*

The Annunciation to the Shepherds (f. 62) is the traditional scene introducing Tierce in the Hours of the Virgin. In this instance, the episode is placed on the right-hand page. For the first time in the manuscript, all marginal figures participate in the action which takes place in the central image. From the top of a small mound, an angel holding a banderole addresses three amazed shepherds. In the margins, five other shepherds, as well as a sixth inside the initial, have heard the message which two other angels have brought them. The two angels seem to have stepped out of the principal scene. Two shepherds express their joy by lifting musical instruments to their mouths; the others are shown in passive or astonished attitudes, while a dog in their midst leaps barking toward the sky.

On the facing page, the procession of *Christ Carrying the Cross* (f. 61v) is passing by. Assisted by Simon of Cyrene, Christ proceeds toward Calvary, carrying the instrument of his torture; he throws a compassionate glance at his Mother, who follows in the company of the Holy Women. Pucelle treats the double movement in this scene with his habitual eurythmy. Among the Jews who are escorting Christ marches the executioner, recognizable by his hammer. One of the two atlantes that hold up the base of the scene's frame is also brandishing a hammer, an allusion to the imminent torture which awaits Christ. Such atlantes were often used as supports in the reliquaries of that time.

The geometrical or plant motifs which embellish the background of the two scenes seem to break through the light layer of color that covers them: a technique which evokes translucid enamel work, again emphasizing the relationship between the present miniatures and goldsmithery.

PLATE 6

THE HOURS OF JEANNE D'ÉVREUX

fol. 68v–69 *The Crucifixion* and *The Adoration of the Magi*

This double page is one of the most outstanding in the entire manuscript. We are at the beginning of Sext, and, in keeping with tradition, Pucelle represents the scene of *The Adoration of the Magi* (f. 69). However, a number of iconographic details distinguish Pucelle's interpretation. The most striking is the nudity of the Christ Child, standing on unstable little legs on the Virgin's lap. This nudity most probably echoes the nudity of the crucified Christ on the facing page, and was unprecedented at the time, even in Italy; only toward the end of the 14th century does it make its regular appearance in the Epiphany and in other scenes from Christ's Infancy. Behind the Virgin and the Magi, five tiny angel musicians stand out against a red background, celebrating the event with a concert.

The episode shown inside the illustrated initial is related to the principal scene: the Magi King's stableboy controls his master's nervous horses with a stick. This theme is unknown in the Gospels, but it appears in many illuminations and ivory carvings during the 14th century (Plate 16). In the bottom margin, the artist shows *The Massacre of the Innocents.* At the instigation of a devil in monkey guise, Herod orders the execution of all first-born children of that year. A mother vainly tries to wrest her son from a soldier who is about to kill him. Another prostrate mother weeps over the death of her child.

The Crucifixion (f. 68v) on the facing page, together with *The Arrest of Christ* (Plate 3), is one of the rare scenes that has not been set inside a frame; it is, moreover, the only scene to spread over the entire page. Two groups are gathered in the foreground, on both sides of the central group composed of Christ and the Two Thieves. On the left, Saint John and the Holy Women are bending over the swooning Virgin whom they catch in mid-fall. This is the well-known theme of the *spasimo* which first gained popularity in Italy during the 14th century; Pucelle's interpretation is one of the first in northern France. On the right, a group of Jews and soldiers are contemplating Christ; the attitudes of several of the personages reflect their equivalents in the Crucifixion of Duccio's *Maestà,* from which Pucelle probably drew the inspiration for his composition. But Pucelle has treated the subject in a manner all his own: the elegant, sinewy graphic style of the groups at the feet of Christ and the Two Thieves remains faithful to the Parisian tradition.

5

6

PLATE 7

The Hours of Jeanne d'Évreux

fols. 82v–83 *The Lamentation over the Body of Christ* and *The Flight into Egypt*

The usual illustration for the beginning of Vespers is *The Flight into Egypt* (f. 83). Like actors, Saint Joseph and the donkey enter and wink at the accomplice spectator. The skeptical, malicious expression of the donkey recalls the meaning of this animal in medieval interpretations: the donkey was supposed to symbolize the stubbornness of the Jews, and was likened to the Old Testament, whereas the bull was considered to be the symbol of the New Testament. Only the Virgin seems to be completely absorbed in her Son, whom she holds tenderly in her arms. The light-blue background is covered with oak branches which form boughs alive with fantastic animals.

The episodes shown in the lower margin are related to the principal scene, but are apocryphal: they are the Idols of the Temple of Hermopolis which crumbled as the Virgin and the Child passed by them, and the Miracle of the Ripe Wheat, which enabled the fugitives to escape Herod's pursuing soldiers. In the initial *D,* formed by two human faces seen in profile, a monkey holds a flaming vessel, while a hybrid being, which forms the tail of the *D,* blows upon the flames with a bellows. In the right-hand margin, another hybrid being, half bishop—half dragon, is playing the harp.

As in the cases of *The Annunciation* and *The Crucifixion,* Pucelle most probably drew his inspiration for the scene on the facing page from a Duccio model. It marks an innovation in northern iconography insofar as the traditional *Anointing of the Dead Christ* has been replaced by the Italo-Byzantine concept of *The Lamentation over the Body of Christ.* Saint John and Joseph of Arimathea have lain Christ's body on a tomb. The Virgin is tenderly embracing the head of her Son, a repetition of her gesture in *The Flight into Egypt.* In the foreground, Mary Magdalene is cleansing the wounds on the right arm of the crucified Christ. In the background, the three Holy Women take part in *The Lamentation:* two are veiled, while the one in the center is wringing her hands, which she raises to heaven, in sign of mourning. Four cherubs which flutter overhead also express their grief: one of them is lying on his back and seems to be tearing his hair. Pucelle's composition is denser than Duccio's, which gives his image greater emotional impact. Two hybrid beings support, not without difficulty, the heavy burden of this scene.

PLATE 8

The Hours of Jeanne d'Évreux

fols. 102v–103 *Queen Jeanne d'Évreux at the Tomb of Saint Louis* and *The Education of Saint Louis*

With his canonization in 1297, King Louis X of France, known as Saint Louis, became the object of a fervent cult in the royal family. A special office in his honor was incorporated in many Missals and Breviaries. But only a small number of Books of Hours contain a liturgical office consecrated to Saint Louis. Two of these were composed for descendents of the Saint: namely, *The Book of Hours of Jeanne d'Évreux* and that of her sister-in-law, Jeanne de Navarre.

In Jeanne d'Évreux's manuscript, the cycle of Saint Louis opens with a double miniature which follows the arrangement of the preceding office of the Virgin. On the left (f. 102v), Pucelle accomplished one of his most daring compositions, and reveals his interest in perspective: the scene represents the interior of a church, adorned with pinnacles and a small bell tower. Queen Jeanne d'Évreux is seen through an arched door, kneeling on her *prie-dieu,* reading her Hours in front of a statue of Saint Louis on a pedestal. The two soldiers seated at the foot of the statue represent guards whom the monks of Saint-Denis were obliged to hire, at the end of the 13th century, to protect the reliquary with the King's remains from the excesses of popular piety. Two atlantes support the structure, which seems to be hanging in mid-air: they are, in turn, supported by two hybrids.

On the right-hand page (f. 103), we see the first in a series of eight scenes taken from the life of Saint Louis. On the whole, these scenes are taken from edifying feats reported by one of the King's biographers, Guillaume de Saint-Pathus. The episode chosen for Matins depicts King Louis accepting chastisement from his confessor, the Dominican Geoffroy de Beaulieu. In this instance Pucelle did not repeat his ingenious spatial tour de force of the preceding page. A door, which is curiously attached to the reliquary frame of the scene, symbolizes the entrance to the royal residence. A soldier stands guard in front of it, and two other soldiers appear below, in the initial and in the bough of leaves which prolongs the initial. With his club, one of them seems to be threatening a hybrid being, half woman–half animal, inside the initial. At the very bottom, a musician carried by a bearded hybrid dreamily plays the viol. In the right-hand margin, three other figures seem to be engaged in a quarrel.

7

PLATE 9

THE HOURS OF JEANNE D'ÉVREUX

fols. 154v–155 *Saint Louis: The Miraculous Return of his Breviary* and *Decorated Text Page*

With Lauds, the illustration of the Hours of Saint Louis begins to follow a different layout: from this point on the image occupies the left-hand page only, while merely decorative elements or drolleries appear amid the text on the facing page.

In this instance, the miraculous episode has not been taken from Guillaume de Saint-Pathus, but from the *Grandes Chroniques de France.* Saint Louis had lost his Breviary in the course of the battle of Damiette, and then became a prisoner of the Saracens. He was mourning the loss when the book was miraculously returned to him by divine intervention. Saint Louis is shown inside a fortress, in the company of a monk who witnessed the miracle (f. 154v). Two round towers with double crowns frame the gate to the citadel, whose walls are reinforced with square towers. The strongly plastic treatment of the fortress seems to project it outside the framework of goldsmithery in which it is encased. Two Saracen guards support the entablature.

The facing page of text (f. 155), begins with the initial *D,* composed of living elements, a revival of a Romanesque formula which enjoyed renewed success in the 14th century. Two bearded profiles compose the loop of the letter to which clings a personage, the body ending in the shoot of a plant. Inside the letter, an amply draped hybrid being is seen playing the viol. In the lower margin, a bagpipe player and a hybrid who is swinging a bell, his face hidden under a pointed bonnet, seem to be trying to rouse the sleeping Saracens. The figures at the ends of various lines are but examples of the inexhaustible imagination which Pucelle used to enliven the text pages of the manuscript.

PLATE 10

The Hours of Jeanne d'Évreux

fols. 159v–160 *Saint Louis Burying the Bones of the Crusaders* and *Decorated Text Page*

Another edifying incident from the life of Saint Louis has been used to illustrate the beginning of Nones. In 1253 the Saracens had taken the city of Sidon and massacred over two thousand Christians. When the city was reconquered by the Crusaders, Saint Louis helped to bury the dead.

The King is seen placing a skull into a sack already filled with skulls which a masked, bonneted gravedigger is holding out to him (f. 159v). The man averts his face and the King's companions hold their noses to escape the stench which rises from the charnel field: these are all details which can be found in Guillaume de Saint-Pathus's biography. Here, too, Pucelle has introduced an architectural element treated in *alto relievo*. An extra decoration of foliage stands out against a background streaked with lines in red ink.

The initial *D* of the text on the facing page (f. 160) is composed of foliage. A cross-legged maniac bites savagely into a leafy branch which curls away from the rest. The face of the mourning half-figure at his feet is completely covered with a drapery.

Inside the initial, a personage is stabbing a hybrid with a sword. A similar subject appears in the lower margin. In spite of the grotesque treatment, these figures may perhaps allude to the massacres at Sidon. Two rabbits are seen playing on the page. In the Middle Ages these animals were synonymous with fertility and their presence in this context may perhaps mean the perpetual struggle of life against death. The monk seen from the back, raising a chalice, is one of the many motifs of this Book of Hours which the Duke Jean de Berry had copied for his *Grandes Heures* (Bibl. Nat., Ms. Lat. 919).

9

10

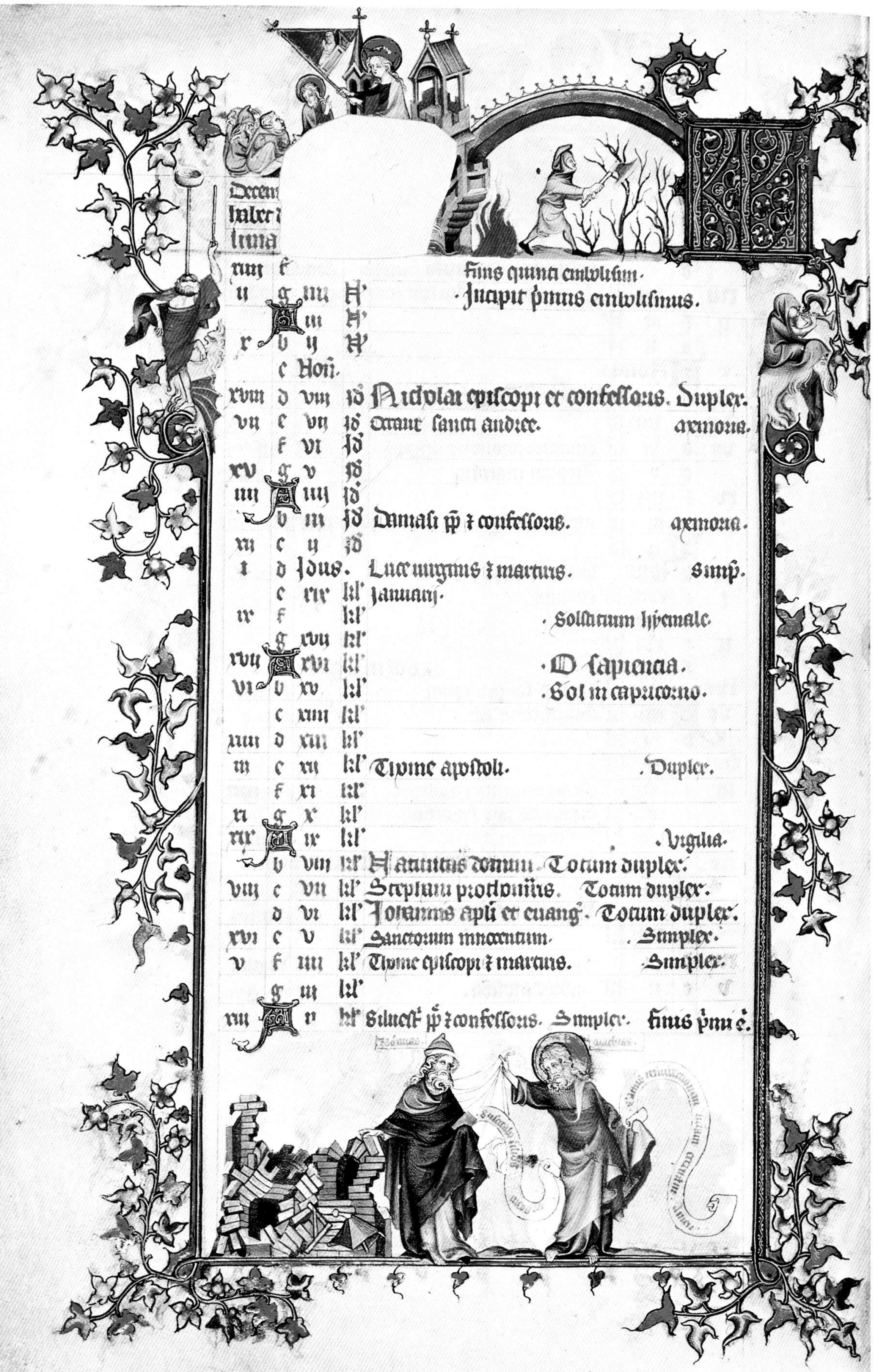
Fins quinti embolismi.
Incipit primus embolismus.
Nicholai episcopi et confessoris. Duplex.
Octave sancti andree. Memoria.
Damasi pp & confessoris. Memoria.
Lucie virginis & martiris. simp.
Januarii.
Solsticium hyemale.
O sapiencia.
Sol in capricorno.
Thome apostoli. Duplex.
Vigilia.
Nativitas domini. Totum duplex.
Stephani prothomartiris. Totum duplex.
Johannis apostoli et evang. Totum duplex.
Sanctorum innocentium. Simplex.
Thome episcopi & martiris. Simplex.
Silvestri pp & confessoris. Simplex. Finis primi

11

PLATE 11

The Belleville Breviary

Tome I, fol. 6v *December*

Like many manuscripts of this type, *The Belleville Breviary* consists of two volumes, one for the summer section of the divine office, and the other for the winter section. Footnotes indicate that a number of collaborators were invited to work on the decoration of the Breviary, with Pucelle appearing to be the overall creator of the work.

Two highly original iconographic cycles illustrate the Calendar and the Psalter. In both cases Pucelle probably followed the directions of a Dominican theologian for his concept; both cycles are explained in an "account of the personages whose images appear in the calendar and in the psalter" (Ms. Lat. 10483, fols. 2–4). A reading of the text reveals that two full-page paintings of a symbolical subject had been inserted between the Calendar and the Psalter in the first volume. Unfortunately, these two paintings have been lost. Although only the months of November and December have been preserved in *The Belleville Breviary*, the original cycle of the Calendar can, nonetheless, be reconstructed in its entirety, thanks to the numerous copies that were made of it in various royal manuscripts during the 14th century.

The basic idea was to prove "the concordance of the Old Testament with the New." For this purpose, the artist has placed a prophet (in this case Zachariah), and an apostle (in this case Matthew), in the bottom margin of each page of the Calendar. The prophet hands a prophecy wrapped in a cloth to the apostle, which the latter unveils, thereby transforming it into an Article of Faith. A building rising behind the prophet represents The Synagogue. Each prophet removes a stone from the Synagogue which he hands to the apostle. At the end of the twelve-month cycle, the Synagogue is shown completely in ruins.

The city gates (unfortunately cut out of the present double page) in the upper part of the Calendar are reminders that the Articles of Faith were "the way and the gate." The Virgin "by whom the door was opened unto us" holds a pennant with a painted image symbolizing the Article of Faith set forth by the apostle at the bottom of the page. At the foot of the gates, Saint Paul addresses various nations (in this case the Hebrews). The didactic cycle above is completed by the more usual cycles of the Zodiac signs and of the months. For the month of December, a peasant is shown clipping the branches of a fruit tree. The Zodiac sign at the bottom of the gate is missing. Two grotesques appear in the upper extremities of the plant shoots which frame the page: they are again characteristic of Pucelle's talent of observation and of his verve.

PLATE 12

The Belleville Breviary

Tome I, fol. 37 *Confirmation*

As in the Calendar, the illustrations of the Psalter in the two volumes of *The Belleville Breviary* deviate from traditional iconography. Instead of the literal system of illustration used in Parisian Psalters since the 13th century, the present manuscript deals with the theme of the sacraments in a cycle which, according to the text of the "account," had been announced by the two lost full-page paintings which followed the end of the Calendar. This sacramental cycle was limited to the seven first divisions of the Psalter and ended at Psalm 109 with an eschatological vision of the *Last Judgment*. This image, too, has disappeared from *The Belleville Breviary*, but it is known from the copy made of it for *The Breviary of Charles V* (Plate 37).

The sacrament chosen as the companion piece for the beginning of Psalm 69 is that of Confirmation, symbolized, in the center of the lower margin, by a young boy receiving the unction from the hands of a bishop. As was characteristic of the predilection for antithetical settings in the Middle Ages, this little scene is framed by a virtue on one side and by its opposing vice on the other. In this case, Strength, on the right, represented standing on a lion, is connected with the Confirmation. Opposing it, a scene from the Bible shows Delilah cutting off Samson's hair, symbolizing Weakness and Cowardice. We learn from the text of the "account" that the vice has been placed on the left as an indication that one must be aware of the "way on the left (the sinister way) which is lined with the seven vices which oppose the virtues." There is also a subtle relationship between the illustration at the beginning of Psalm 69 and the subject of the sacraments. Instead of the traditional David in the Waters, beseeching the Lord, the present illustration shows Saint Peter, lying in a boat tossed about by the waves, imploring the help of the Lord who blesses him from the clouds. This scene has no historical value: its meaning is clearly allegorical, Saint Peter's boat symbolizing the Church. It is the theme of the soul's fortitude in times of trial, of the Church's trust in God in spite of tribulations. Three grotesque figures in the right margin introduce an element of gaiety to the austerity of this didactic program.

93

Luxure tout le cors & lame
Et si tout dieu & nre dame
Son domage a bien en tachie
Qui same pert por tel vuachie
Vachiez est ce ce nest pas doute
Car lame suelle & honnist toute
Por ce vous nous dit saite escripture
Fuiez fuiez fuiez luxure
Fuions la tuit fuions fuions
Ne cuer ne cors ni apuions
Qui si aert qui si apuie
Le porcel resemble & la truie
Quant pl' se soille & pl' sen boe
Tant li siet plus & plaist la boe
En fiens & en bourbier habite
Qui se soille qui si delite
En lorde boe de luxure
Qui son cuer i met & sa cure
Bien est semblant a la quanete
Qui toute ior bourte & bourbete
Bourbetant va sanz destourbier

Versificator: Blanditur menti luxurie ta libido fauen[s]

La gloire la glorieuse
Une miracle merveilleuse
Ancois vous vueil en
cor retraire
Qua rime vueille na
port traire
La mere dieu tel vent menoit

13A

Por ce que tout giulent & boulent
En enfer ardent tuit & boulent
Du vilain qui agnt poine savoit
La moitie de son ave maria.

Conter vous vueil
sans nul delai
Un miracle dun
homme lai
Ou il a mlt a mer
veillier.
Et mlt's genz doit esveillier
A honourer la clere gemme
La sainte ...

Volentiers bones trespassoit
Nus labeurs ne le lessoit
En tel estoit de lui acrivistre
Tant lourdas vilain tant enclostre
Et tant sottart avoit en lui
Que peu amez iert de nului
De laborer en tel estoit
Que povrement festes festoit
Et ne pourquant tant vous en di
La puis none le samedi.
Ne laboureist por nule paine
Et volentiers le diemaine
Oit la messe & le servise
Et la lettre qui le devise
Et ia soit ce que mlt fust lordes
Et quanqu'il fust roides & gordes
Come un bestor ou une eschame
Devant lymage nre dame
Sagenoilloit assez souvent
Nourris nestoit pas en couvent
Car ne seut pas par un apostre
Qui seust nes sa paternostre
Mais il avoit tant esploitie
Ne sai le tiers ou la moitie
Savoit du salu nre dame
Que li avoit apris sa fame.
Ciert ses mains & ses quanques

Versificator dicit: Cum tua non metis metis ...

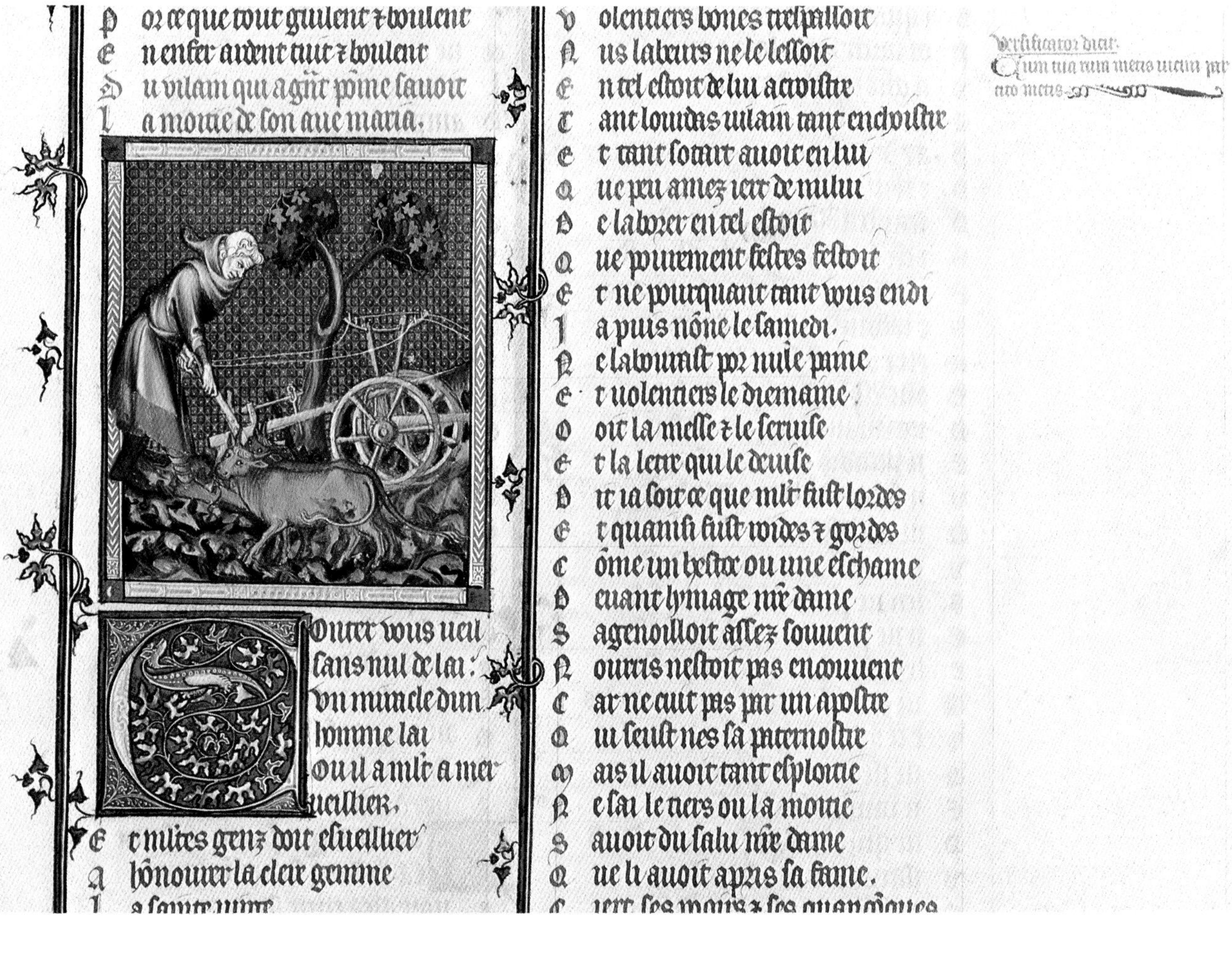

13B

PLATE 13

THE MIRACLES OF OUR LADY

A. fol. 93 *The Abduction of the Little Nun*

As indicated in the title, this work is a compilation of fifty-eight episodes in eight-syllable verse that relate the miracles which the Virgin performed for a number of her faithful worshippers. Each miracle is preceded by a miniature which fills the width of a column of text; a large full-page miniature, representing the Virgin seated on Solomon's throne, serves as frontispiece to the volume. The whole series is obviously the work of Pucelle.

The scene represented here illustrates the story of "The Little Nun Who Left Her Convent and Walked Off Into The Century." A nun who was particularly devoted to Our Lady had been seduced by a young nobleman who wished to marry her. She decided to leave her convent, but succeeded only during her third attempt, when she failed to kneel before the statue of the Virgin. Thirty years later, the Virgin appeared to her in a dream and convinced her to take the veil again, her husband becoming a monk. The miniature depicts the abduction scene. Sitting on a brown horse which she is prodding with a whip, the nun escapes from her convent, at the urgent promptings of an elegant young nobleman. As in his other works, Pucelle reveals his interest in tactile impression and in the third dimension, as can be seen in the admirable drapery of the nun's robe.

B. fol. 172 *The Laborer and his Plow*

This miracle is called: "About The Villain Who Painstakingly Learned One-Half of His Hail Mary." An ignorant laborer could learn only one-half of the Hail Mary which his wife had tried to teach him. Moved by the sincere devotion which the man manifested on her behalf, the Virgin saved him from damnation just as the devil was about to carry him off. The miniature shows the laborer with his plow, from which he has unyoked two oxen. The almost monochrome scene is a wonderful variation of browns and maroons. The artist's rendering of the quality of plowed-up earth is particularly successful, and his reproduction of the plow has great technical interest. The pictorial execution is extremely free, not to say daring, as shown by the strong accent of white on one of the branches of the tree.

PLATE 14

The Geneva Bible Historiale

fol. I *Christ in Majesty*

The text of this manuscript enjoyed great popularity at the end of the Middle Ages, and has come down to us in many copies: it is a French translation of the Bible, with interpolated passages from the *Historia Ecclesiastica* by Pierre Comestor; the translation by Guyart des Moulins, Canon of Saint-Pierre d'Aire in the Diocese of Thérouanne, took four years to complete: from 1291 to 1294.

Since they are so numerous, the illustrations of *Bibles Historiales* are often not carefully executed, and thus can be of mediocre quality. This is not the case in the present volume, which begins with a remarkable painting. In the center of a large gothic tabernacle reminiscent of a goldsmith's shrine, we see *Christ in Majesty,* holding an open book in His left hand while bestowing blessings with His right. Standing out against a background of ultramarine-blue foliage, He sits enthroned inside a mandorla with three-colored borders, supported by a choir of angels clothed in pink, mauve, and shades of red. The Evangelists appear on two levels on either side, together with their symbols. Christ's robe is done in *grisaille,* as are those of the Evangelists. A double hunting scene takes place in the lower margin: on the left, the horn sounds the death of the stag, while, on the right, a villain armed with bow and arrow is shooting a hare which his dog has dislodged.

Because of the style and the exquisite refinement of the execution, Pucelle's name has often been mentioned in connection with the present work. But we believe that the creator of this painting is not the master himself, but one of his closest disciples, the artist of *The Breviary of Charles V,* probably the illuminator Jean Le Noir. Taught by Pucelle, and influenced by his style, Le Noir nonetheless distinguished himself by a more lyrical feeling for form and by a livelier, less monumental treatment of the human body, which link him beyond his teacher with certain followers of Honoré (Plate 2). This development is already noticeable in the paintings of *The Geneva Bible,* one of the earliest works, together with *The Hours of Jeanne de Navarre* (Plates 15–17), wherein the artist's style affirms itself.

The artist has repeated the figure of *Christ in Majesty* from the present Bible in one of his paintings for *The Petites Heures* of Jean de Berry, the last of his known works (Plate 39).

Prologe
Ci commence la bible hystori
aus ou les hystores escolastres
cest li prohemes celui qui
mist cest livre du latin en
francois.
Pour ce que li deables
qui chascun iour e
presche destorbe et
enordist les cuers
des homes par oiseuse et par
cil las que il a tendus pour
nous prendre entre nos cuers
come celui qui onques ne cesse
de agaitier coment il nous
puist amener a peche pour
nos ames traire en son puant
enfer avecques lui. et il est
mestier a nous clers et prestres
de sainte eglise qui devons est
re lumiere du monde que nos
apres nos heures et nos orai
sons entendons a aucune bo
ne oeuvre faire. si que li peres des
dampnez li deables come il
nous vient assaillir de ses tem
tations et nos truisse oiseus
par quoi il ait achoison de legie
rement entrer en nos cuers et
face cheoir en pechie premiere
ment par pensee et apres par o
euvre. Si devons seur toute riens
fuir oiseuse et entendre a bien
faire et oeuvre qui plaise a dieu
et au deable soit contraire. Et
pour ce que li deables qui molt de
fois ma fait pechier par oiseu
se ne me puist mais trouver
mes tous iours esloigniez dau
cune bone oeuvre. Et ie qui sui pre
stres et chanoines de s. pere dai
re de leveschie de terouane. Et
Guiars des moulins sui apelez
premierement a la louenge de
dieu et de la beneoite vierge
marie et de tous sains et apres
au profit de tous ceus qui ces
te oeuvre verront. et a la requeste
dun mien especial ami qui
molt desire le profit de mame
translate les livres hystoriaus
de la bible de latin en francois
que li maistres en traite les hy
stoires les escolastres en lais
sant des hystoires ce dont il nest
nul mestiers de translater. et
en faisant premierement le ti
extre des livres hystoriaus de
la bible. Si pri a trestous ce
ulz qui ces translations verront
que sil a aucune chose a repren
dre de lordenance du rommans
que il maient pour escuse. quar
seur laine de moi ie ni ai nes
uns ni adiouste fors tant
seulement pour verite si come
ie lai ou latin de la bible trov
ue et des hystores les escolastres
Et qui les vendroit regarder
leu y porroit tout certainement
trouver la pure verite de tou
tes ces translations coment
ie lai trait du latin mot a
mot si come ie le raconte. Si
rent graces a dieu de lespasse
de vie et de la sante et de tant

PLATE 15

The Hours of Jeanne de Navarre

fol. 53 *The Annunciation to the Shepherds*

In spite of a close kinship with Pucelle, the paintings by the best of the three artists who collaborated on the first campaign of illustrations in this Book of Hours display original traits. These allow us to identify their creator as the illuminator Jean Le Noir. Jean Le Noir was, in all probability, the Pucellian artist who illustrated *The Breviary of Charles V* (Plate 37) and part of *The Petites Heures* of Jean de Berry (Plate 39). Two of the most important cycles in *The Hours of Jeanne de Navarre,* the cycle of the Hours of the Virgin and that of the Hours of the Passion, are decidedly his. It is doubtful that Jean Le Noir could have been the creator of the masterplan in *The Hours of Jeanne de Navarre* before 1334, the year in which his teacher Pucelle died. Nevertheless, Pucelle's ghost still haunts the manuscript in a number of places, including the Calendar, which is a scrupulous reproduction of the Calendar in the first volume of *The Belleville Breviary,* and certain details of the paintings, such as the margins.

A scene such as *The Annunciation to the Shepherds* is a particularly revealing example of those traits which link and those which separate the disciple from the master. The composition would be inconceivable without the precedent of *The Hours of Jeanne d'Évreux* (Plate 5), from which Jean Le Noir has borrowed a number of elements, a practice he continues in his later works: extending the scene of *The Annunciation to the Shepherds* beyond the limits of the main painting into the margins is an idea he owes to Pucelle. The pensive shepherd in the right margin is an outright copy of one of Pucelle's shepherds, while the cape-wearing shepherd accompanied by a dog is partly based on a similar figure in the Cloisters manuscript. The lower half of the seated shepherd who is playing the bombardon in the main painting follows Pucelle's model in *The Hours of Jeanne d'Évreux* fold by fold.

Le Noir distinguishes himself very clearly from his teacher, however, by the stockier mold of his figures, with their heavier, almost bloated faces, as well as by the harmonious, practically musical rhythm of his compositions which differ considerably from the more structured style of Pucelle. The artist has tried to give an impression of depth by placing two of the shepherds behind a mound of terrain, a "gimmick" which he repeats in two later mansucripts, *The Hours of Yolande of Flanders* and *The Petites Heures* of Jean de Berry.

Like all the paintings in this manuscript, the scene is placed inside a multilobed frame with a three-colored border, a pattern which will be used frequently during the reign of Charles V (Plates 32–33).

cede. p dnm nrm ihm xpm filium tuu. qui te
cum uiuit et regnat in unitate spiritus sancti
deus p omnia secula seculorum. Amen. Do
mine exaudi orationem meam. Et clamor
meus ad te ueniat. Benedicamus domino.
Deo gracias. Anime omnium fidelium defunc
torum p misericordiam dei requiescant i pace am.

PLATE 16

The Hours of Jeanne de Navarre

fol. 55v *The Adoration of the Magi*

Jean Le Noir illustrates the Office of Sext in the Hours of the Virgin with the traditional scene of *The Adoration of the Magi.* The image appears as though seen through a window, which is formed by the three-colored quatrefoil which serves as the frame: one of the points of the quatrefoil extends over the upper arm of the King on the left, which gives an impression of depth. The personages stand out against a delicately executed background composed of poly-foiled shapes, within which lion masks alternate with diamond-pointed stones.

As on the preceding page, elements of the main scene have been dropped to the lower margin: for instance the stableboy whipping the horses of the Magi Kings, a motif which we also encountered in *The Adoration of the Magi* in *The Hours of Jeanne d'Évreux* (Plate 6). To the right, a lady in prayer, obviously Jeanne de Navarre, the person for whom the manuscript was commissioned, seems to take part in the scene; this is a first step toward the integration of contemporary personages into *The Adoration*, a custom which spread during the 15th century; Gozzoli's cycle of the Magi in the Palazzo Medici in Florence being its most famous example. Various grotesque figures and a number of particularly well-rendered birds animate the margins: going from top to bottom, a goldfinch, a green woodpecker, and a swallow are clearly recognizable. Jean Le Noir and his workshop seem to have been particularly fond of placing birds in the margins; this became the custom in Parisian manuscripts beginning in the middle of the 14th century.

Compared to the same subject in *The Hours of Jeanne d'Évreux, The Adoration of the Magi* in *The Hours of Jeanne de Navarre* shows noticeable differences: Le Noir prefers the dynamic element created by a diagonal composition to his predecessor's vertical-block scansion. Almost folded into the ground, the kneeling Magi King forms a pyramid with the Christ Child who is leaning toward him, while the Child's movement is extended by the gesture of the other King, who is bending backward, pointing to the star of Bethlehem.

PLATE 17

THE HOURS OF JEANNE DE NAVARRE

fol. 109 *The Arrest of Christ on Mount Olivet*

In *The Arrest of Christ on Mount Olivet,* which opens the Hours of the Passion in *The Hours of Jeanne de Navarre,* Jean Le Noir clearly admits his debt to Pucelle: his composition repeats that of Pucelle in *The Hours of Jeanne d'Évreux* (Plate 3). Le Noir did, however, add a number of details of a picturesque and anecdotal character: the hideous faces of the Jewish soldiers express the wickedness of their souls, Christ throws Judas a look filled with bitterness and pain; Saint Peter has become a boorish type with a stubborn forehead, while, at his feet, Malchus has been transformed into a grimacing Negro. Nothing is left of the noble reserve of Pucelle's scene in this group torn by conflicting passions.

In the lower margin, a young man is hiding in a bush; this is probably an allusion to the young man mentioned in the Gospel of Saint Mark who fled at the moment the event occurred. Saint Mark specifies that the young man had to flee naked because his tunic had been torn from his body. In the present image, the artist has transformed the scene: through the screen of leaves the young man stares at the boot which he had been forced to abandon during his flight.

An element from the main scene reappears in the illustrated initial: the soldier who is looking toward the spectators from under his half-raised visor. This motif is one of Pucelle's inventions (Plate 3), which Jean Le Noir repeated some forty years later in the corresponding scene in *The Petites Heures* of Jean de Berry (Plate 39).

ci commencent les heures de la croiz
omine labia mea aperies
t os meum annunciabit lau
dem tuam
eus in adiutorium meum intende
omine ad adiuuandum me festi

PLATE 18

The Psalter of Bonne de Luxembourg

A. fols. 83v–84 *Psalm 52* and *Decorated Text Page*

Three paintings in particular stand out from the totality of the work. The first (f. 83v) is the illustration which introduces Psalm 52: "*Dixit insipiens in corde suo non est Deus . . .*" In this instance, the fool usually illustrating this psalm has been completely transformed. An anti-Semitic inspiration is evident in the image showing a figure beating and pulling at the hood of a Jew who seems to be drinking from something resembling a chalice. The strongly Semitic profile of the Jew, who symbolizes the fool, is also found elsewhere in the manuscript in an entirely different context: in the Janus illustrating the month of January. The two figures executed in *grisaille* stand out against a background of monochrome blue decorated with boughs and grotesques. In the lower margin, two small lions gnawing on a bone frame the Arms of Bonne of Luxembourg which are hanging from a tree. A variety of birds, rendered with ornithological precision, perch in the leaf branches of the frame.

B. fols. 321v–322 *The Three Living* and *The Three Dead*

The lively scene shown on these two pages illustrates the well-known story of *The Three Living* and *The Three Dead,* the title of a moral "fable," five poetic versions of which have been traced back to the second half of the 13th century. In *The Psalter of Bonne of Luxembourg,* the encounter of *The Three Living* and *The Three Dead* forms a contrasting diptych. On the left (f. 321v), the three young noblemen on horseback form an agitated group: The first rider, who is wearing a crown, is horrified by the dreadful vision and tries to turn back; the companion next to him points his index finger in the directon of the three corpses while trying to protect himself from the stench which emanates from them. The third rider makes a gesture of surprise. The skillful tangle of the horses and the agitated drapery are a perfect expression of the shock felt by the group. At the end of the plant shoot on the left, a hooded personage buries his nose in his coat, apparently taking part in the scene.

The rigid, petrified attitude of the three "frozen" figures on the facing page (f. 322) contrasts with the gesticulations of the Living. All three corpses are shown standing, in varying degrees of decomposition; the skeleton farthest to the right hardly has any flesh left on its bones. Monochrome backgrounds with exquisitely painted motifs emphasize the various participants. The usual repertory of birds animates these two folios, which are among the most successful in the volume.

18 A

18B

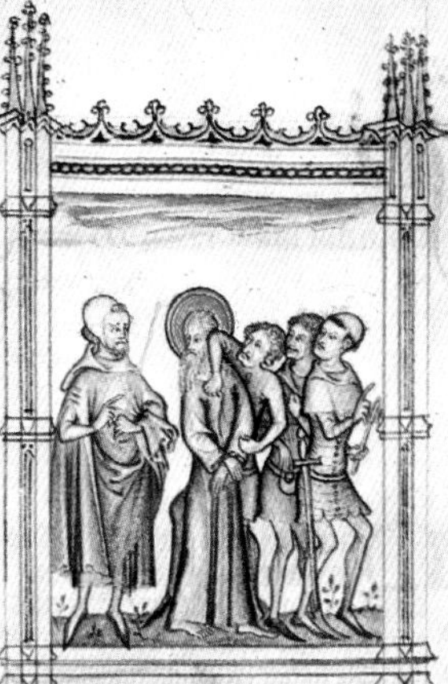

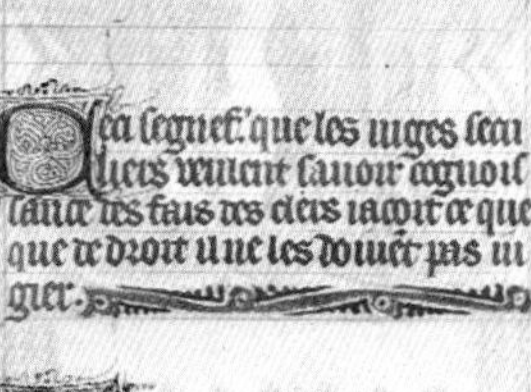

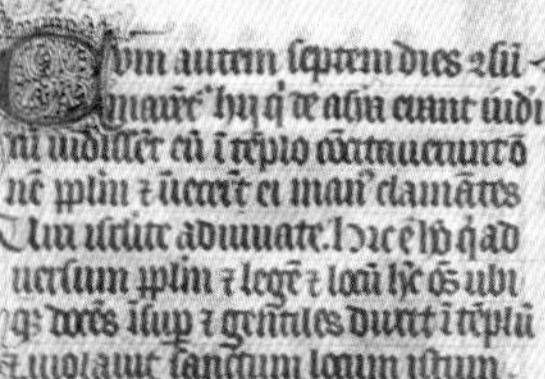

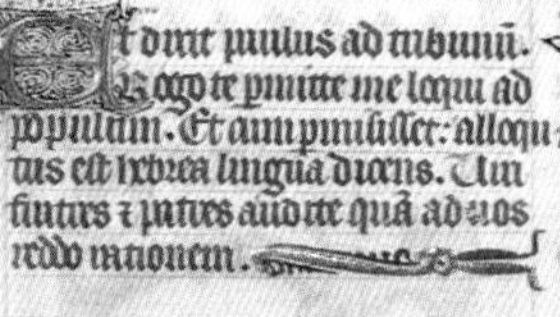

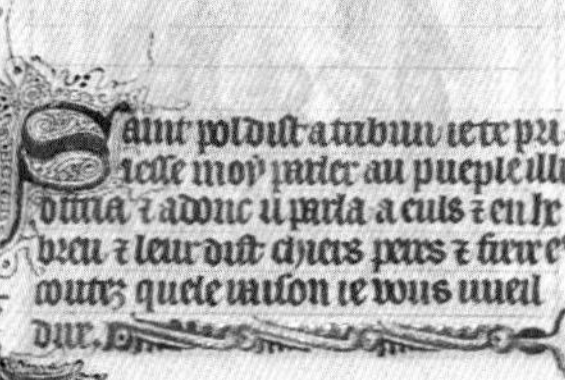

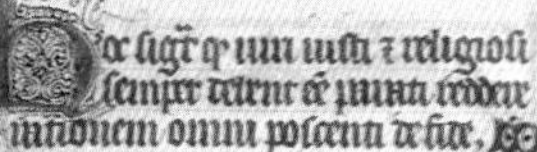

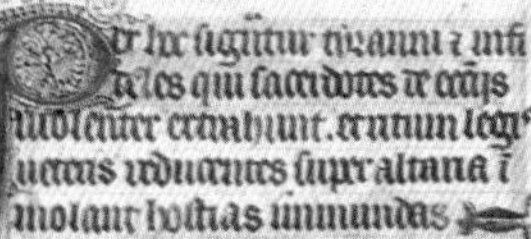

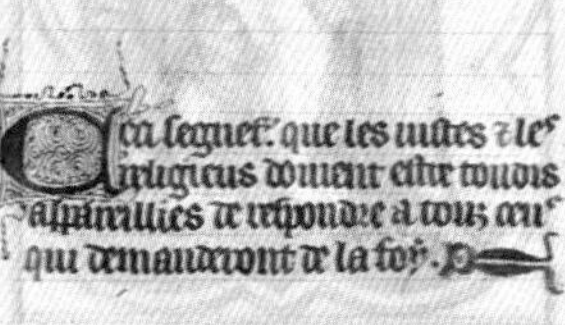

PLATE 19

The Bible Moralisée of Jean le Bon

fol. 285v *The Life of Saint Paul*

The 5122 illustrations in this Bible, all treated in *grisaille*, are a veritable treasure chest for students of Parisian illumination in the middle of the 14th century; they are the result of the collaboration of some fifteen different artists, a certain number of whom already show a remarkable tendency toward the naturalism which characterized the second half of the 14th century. The present page is the work of one of these innovators. The four Biblical illustrations are distinguished from the "moral" images by an architectural frame which is reminiscent of the miniatures in *The Hours of Jeanne d'Évreux* (Plates 4–10). All four refer to an episode from the life of Saint Paul as told in the Acts of the Apostles (21, 23–40). While on a mission to Jerusalem, Saint Paul heeds the request of the leaders of the Christian community and accompanies four of their members to the temple for a purification rite (Scene 1). He is recognized by the Jews who accuse him of profaning their temple; they expel him from the temple and threaten to kill him (Scene 2). He is bound with chains and interrogated by the Roman tribune (Scene 3). Saint Paul asks the tribune to allow him to justify himself before the Jews (Scene 4).

The illustrations of the "moralities" are set inside elongated poly-lobes. Saint Paul's preaching is likened to Confession and to the predication of the Doctors of the Church, and the arrest of the Apostle parallels the persecutions suffered by the Church. Saint Paul's appearance before the Roman tribunal is interpreted as the abuse, by laymen, of the jurisdiction of the Church, while his address is interpreted as the justification of the Faith.

The creator of these illustrations is the same artist who illustrated a manuscript of the works of Guillaume de Machaut (Plates 23–26). Characteristics of his style are: a realistic sharpness in the design, a feeling for volume, and an interest in details of fashion. Although liberated from the influence of Pucelle, his clearly drawn scenes reveal an artist of French temperament.

PLATE 20

The Bible Moralisée of Jean le Bon

fol. 59 *Samson and Delilah*

The four Bible scenes on this page have been taken from the Book of Judges (16, 4–21), and depict the story of Samson betrayed by Delilah: Delilah is shown in the first image, being bribed by the Philistines; in the corresponding "moralization" she is being compared to the bad Christians "who give in to the will of the flesh," which the illustration symbolizes by a group of religious dignitaries, among them a bishop whom demons are pushing toward a prostitute. In the text below, Delilah vainly tries three times to hand Samson over to the Philistines: the illustration shows Delilah's third attempt, rather obscurely told in the Bible, according to which she supposedly tried to drive a peg into her lover's hair. The illustration of the "moral" commentary shows a woman kneeling before Christ, symbolizing the Christian soul escaping from the snares of temptation. In the second illustrated column, Delilah is shown cutting off Samson's hair, while Philistine soldiers under the shelter of a roof prepare to seize him: in the commentary, this passage is likened to the despair of the sinning soul which falls into the hands of the demons. In the final episode, the Philistines put out Samson's eyes and attach him to the millstone. According to the commentary, the blinded Samson represents the sinner who has been deprived of the grace of the Holy Ghost and "is blind to all things of the Spirit," thus succumbing to the temptations of the flesh and to avarice.

Together with the preceding illuminator, the author of this page is one of the most remarkable artists in this Bible. Using finely graded tones of gray he is notable for the expressive vigor of his personages; a certain lack of care as to the proportions may possibly indicate Flemish or Dutch origins. Like the work of Guillaume de Machaut's illustrator, these pictures bear important testimony to the evolution of taste and the appearance of clinging shapes in fashion which began to spread throughout Europe beginning in the middle of the 14th century.

Postea adamavit dalidam et illa prec ad peticionem philistinorum decepit eum.

Apres ces choses sampson ama vne fame qui ot nom dalida et elle le deceut et le baillia en la main de ses ennemis les philistiens.

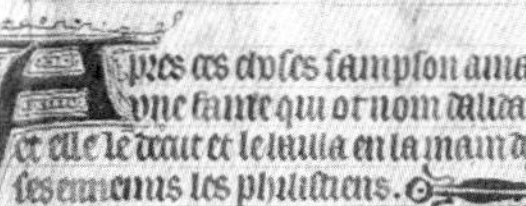

Hec refertur ad aliqua membra christi non ad personam quorum carni consentientes et spiritum ei subicientes decipiuntur et in manu adversariorum traduntur.

Ceci est reporte en figure a ceus qui sunt ou deussent estre membres de ihesucrist et qui ont le nom de crestien qui se consentent a la volente de la char et issousmettent lesperit et est deceu par la char et baillie en la main de lanemi.

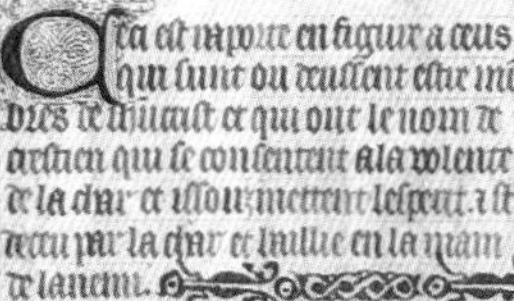

Ter ligavit dalida sampsonem primo septem funibus. secundo novellis. tercio clavo et licio perpillos et semper evasit.

Dalida lia sampson par .iii. fois premierement de .vii. cordes. secondement de .ix. tiercement d'un clou tres fort et bien fichie par ses cheveus et touz ses liens eschapa et rompi.

Hec signat quod caro decipit spiritum per diversa genera peccandi per septem criminalia peccata. postea per consuetudinem et adinventionem novorum et laudatorem peccaminum et postea per superbiam de hiis tamen evadit homo per penitentiam.

Ceci segnefie que la char deceoit lesperit par .iii. manieres de pechez premierement par .vii. principaus pechez mortels. apres par costume et par trouver nouviaus pechez et lors sont .ix. apres par orgueilleuse obstination en son peche qu'il ne daigne demander ne oir parler de son salut et toutevois par repentance et penance eschape len aucune foiz de ces las a.

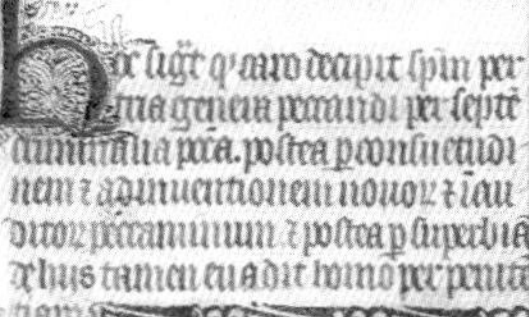

Tercio revelat dalide caput sampsonis et abscidit septem crines et tradidit inimicis suis.

Au darrenier dalida rest les cheveus du chief sampson et en ot .vii. et se departi la force de li et fu baillie en la main des philistiens ses adversaires.

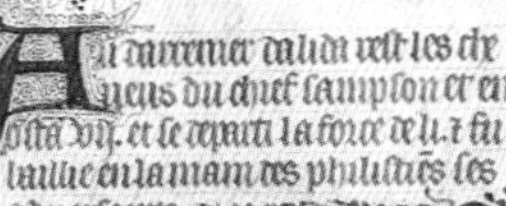

Hec signat quod spiritus seductus carne septem donis spiritus sancti spoliatur et postea cadit in desperationem quod peccatum nunquam dimittatur et ita tradit diabolo et angelis eius.

Ceci segnefie que lesperit deceu par la char est despoillie des .vii. dons du saint esperit et puis chiet le pecheur en desesperance de laquelle il n'est deslie. et puis est baillie en la main des anemis.

Sampson tonsis crinibus excecatur et ad molam ponitur.

Quant sampson ot perdu ses cheveus et sa force len li creva les iex et fu avugle et le mist len a tourner la meule.

Hec signat quod homo peccator spiritus sancti amissa gratia cecus efficitur in spiritualibus et mundi curis et laboribus subiugatur ut carnales et avari.

Ceci segnefie que quant le pecheur a perdu la grace du saint esprit il ne voit goute es choses esperitueles et est du tout occupe es cures et es besoignes du monde comme sont charneus et avaricieus et semblables.

21

PLATE 21

THE MISSAL OF SAINT-DENIS

fol. 256v *The Miracle of the Leprous Pilgrim*

The fact that this manuscript was destined for the Abbey of Saint-Denis explains the illustrations in the volume, depicting two events relative to the founding of the Abbey during the Merovingian era. An illustration in the Office of the Dedication of the Church retraces three phases of a miracle which occurred during the consecration of the Abbey after it was built by Dagobert. The legend tells of a leprous pilgrim who had hidden himself in the church the evening before the official ceremony, and saw Christ appear "*niveis vestibus indutus,*" blessing the different sections of the building and followed by Saint Peter, Saint Paul, and Saint Denis with his companions. After the blessing, Christ spoke to the leper and ordered him to tell Dagobert's bishops not to repeat the consecration ceremony. When the leper asked for proof of what he had just witnessed, Christ seized him by the hair and pulled the festering skin off his body. The next morning, the pilgrim transmitted the divine message to Dagobert and his court, convincing them by displaying his leprous skin.

The pilgrim's vision is depicted in the illustration which precedes the text of the Office: squatting in a niche, the leper watches Christ and His saints walk through the church. In the lower right margin, the story continues with the healing of the leper whose skin Christ is pulling off his face. On the left, the now elegantly clothed pilgrim kneels to Dagobert and his courtiers, showing them his leper's mask as proof of the message he is bringing.

The page is framed by foliage alive with a repertory of birds similar to those in *The Hours of Jeanne de Navarre* and *The Psalter of Bonne de Luxembourg.* However, the style of the missal illustrations is clearly more advanced than in these two manuscripts. Its illuminator is obviously the master who illustrated Machaut's *Le Remède de Fortune* and *Le Dit du Lion* (Plates 23–26).

In spite of its errors in perspective, the apparition scene in the church shows renewed interest in spatial problems which most followers of Pucelle had neglected. It is one of the most daring illustrations of this type since *The Hours of Jeanne d'Évreux.*

PLATE 22

THE MISSAL OF SAINT-DENIS

fol. 261 *Saint Denis Aids Dagobert*

The illustration at the beginning of the Office of the Relics of Saint Denis depicts another episode from Dagobert's life. The scene recalls the events which led to the Merovingian King's devotion to the first Bishop of Paris. During a hunting party in which the young Dagobert took part, a stag sought refuge in the church of Catulliacus which contained the tombs of Saint Denis and his companions. Paralyzed by an invisible power, neither hounds nor hunters were able to enter the church and seize the stag. Shortly thereafter Dagobert had a falling out with his father Clotharius and also took refuge in the same church. He fell asleep on Saint Denis's tomb and had a dream in which the saint and his companions appeared to him; they promised to come to his aid if he built them an edifice worthy of them. After several vain attempts to force his way into the church, Clotharius forgave his son.

The miraculous hunting scene is represented with remarkable skill. The initial *O* at the beginning of the Office merely serves to reinforce the impression of depth, with the action spilling over on all sides. Jumping through the letter as though it were a hoop, the hounds vainly bark at the stag who has taken refuge in the church. This edifice is depicted as a slender building; it is seen from an angle, which emphasizes the effect of depth. One of its pillars cuts daringly into the letter. In the upper margin, a dog comes leaping out of a copse; copses became quite frequent in illuminations during the reign of Charles V.

The decorated initial is proof of considerable progress in scenographic detail; two episodes from the same legend complete the initial in the lower margin: on the left, Saint Denis and his companions appear to the sleeping Dagobert in the church of Catulliacus; on the right, Dagobert is reconciled with his father Clotharius, who has vainly tried to enter the church. Such unenclosed scenes must have contributed greatly to the growing tendency to include landscapes in paintings.

PLATE 23

GUILLAUME DE MACHAUT, LE REMÈDE DE FORTUNE

fol. 23 *The Lover Contemplates his Lady*

This manuscript is one of the outstanding works of 14th-century French illumination. The artist who supplied the best of the illustrations can certainly be considered the most innovative illuminator since Pucelle, and the true creator of that naturalism which began to triumph in French illumination under the reign of Charles V.

Although nothing is known about the owner of the work, a study of the text furnishes chronological data which allow it to be placed around 1350. This is an astonishingly early date, considering the style of the paintings, but it is confirmed by a number of other illuminated manuscripts by the same artist which date from the same period (Plates 19, 21–22). The artist, who seems to have been assisted by at least two collaborators, reserved the illustration of the most important work in the collection for himself. It is a long poem, called *Le Remède de Fortune,* and consists of a succession of scenes from courtly life, in which Machaut describes the anguish of a lover, played by the author himself, who does not dare declare his passion to the lady he loves.

Although not directly related to the text, which starts out with rather general speculations, the first illustration immediately sets the tone of the poem as a whole: it shows Machaut (in all probability), arriving at his lady's castle. Clad in the short, tight costume which came into fashion around 1340, Machaut and his companion, probably his servant in spite of an equally elegant outfit, have stopped a short distance from the castle. The poet stands with crossed arms, apparently absorbed in the contemplation of his lady, who is standing on the perron of the castle, conversing with three of her ladies-in-waiting. All are elegantly corsetted. The building itself is bristling with pinions, turrets, and chimneys, and looks just like a castle out of a fairy tale. The artist uses a great many angles and corners; the receding line of the roofs corresponds to the beautiful vaulted hall, which is seen at an angle and opens behind the lady's back. In spite of obvious errors in perspective, all these elements contribute to a breaking up of space and to the creation of depth. An Italianist element is added by the frail twisted column which supports one of the corners of the castle. The realism, tempered with courtly elegance, in this as well as in the following scenes, marks a decisive turning point in 14th-century taste and art.

Cilz qui veult
Aucun art aprendre.
A .xij. choses
doit entendre.
La premiere est
quil doit eslire.
Celui ou ses cuers miex le tire
Et ou sa nature lencline
Car la chose einsus bien define
Quen veult encontre son gre faire
Quant nature li est contraire
Aimme son maistre. et son mestier
Sus tout. et ce li est mestier
Qui lonneur obeisse et serve
Et ne quide pas quil sasserve
Car sil les aimme il lameront
Et sil les het. il le harront.

Profiter ne puet aucunement
Doctrine receue humblement
Et bien se gart quil continue
Car science einsus retenue
Est et de legier oubliee
Quant elle nest continuee
Soing. penser. desir. et savoir
Ait. si pourra science avoir
Et lentrepreigne en ieune aage
Ains quen malice son courage
Mue. par trop grant cognoissance
Car le droit estat dinnocence
Ressamble proprement la table
Blanche polie. qui est able
A recevoir sans nul contraire
Ce com y veult paindre ou pourtraire.
Et est aussi comme la cire
Qui sueffre dedens li escrire.

PLATE 24

Guillaume de Machaut, Le Remède de Fortune

fol. 51 *The Lover Sings as his Lady Dances*

Machaut has concealed himself in the distant Park of Hesdin, for fear of having to confess that he is the author of a lay which his lady asked him to read. He is bemoaning Love and Fortune, when a woman of the most wondrous beauty comes to comfort him. The woman turns out to be Hope, and after a long argument she convinces Machaut to return to the one he secretly adores.

Machaut returns to the castle, where he finds his lady in her park, dancing a "carole" in joyful company. At her invitation he joins in and when his turn comes he sings a "ballad song." This is the scene shown in the illustration. Encouraged by a glance from the lady, who can be recognized by the pink cap she is wearing on her head, Machaut prepares to sing his virelay. As in the preceding image he is wearing a sword at his side. The scene takes place on a meadow strewn with flowers, under the sparse shade of four trees with long slender trunks. On the right, three newcomers stand watching the scene; one of them is still wearing his travelling coat.

In spite of an "abstract" background, decorated with golden scrolls, there is air and movement in this charming scene, whose various actors disport themselves with naturalness and ease. As in other parts of the manuscript, the artist delights in showing the bizarre details of the costumes of the time.

51

Je li respondi sans demour:
Ma dame vo commandement
Weil faire mais petitement
Me sai de chant entremettre
Mes cest chose quil couvient estre
Puis qui vous plaist lors sans de lay

En commenchay ce virelay.
Que on claimme chancon balladee
Ainssi doit elle estre clamee.
Comment l'amant
Chante em pres
Sa dame.

Dame a vous sans retollir. Dong cuer. pensee. desir. corps et amour.
Comme a toute la millour quon puist choysir. Ne qui vivre
ne morir. puist a ce jour.
Si ne me doit a folour tourner.
Vostre puissez en valour toute.

PLATE 25

Guillaume de Machaut, Le Remède de Fortune

fol. 55 *The Banquet*

The dance is over. The lady and her company return to the castle. After the celebration of the mass, a trumpet announces preparations for the banquet. In a lively passage Machaut describes the milling about of the servants who are attending to their various chores: one is hurrying to the "bread pantry," another to the wine cellar, others are heading for the kitchens. After having their hands washed by their valets, the gentlemen take their places in the spacious hall, and the feast begins. It ends with a concert and Machaut takes great delight in enumerating the different instruments of the musicians.

The liveliness of the illustrations rivals that of the poem: the gentlemen and the ladies are seated at two separate tables in a spaciously proportioned hall. Their servants bustle about them: cup bearers and meat carvers present beverages and meats to the lady of the house who can be recognized by her cap; another carver kneels before the gentlemen's table, wiping the large blade of his knife with a napkin. In the aisle between the tables, another servant, arms outstretched, carries a platter piled high with fowl. Two bagpipe players and two trumpeters in the background depict the concert which ends the meal.

Here, too, the artist has found occasion to manifest his interest in space. In the castle interior, techniques such as the protrusion of the wall on the left effectively contribute to the impression of depth, while the receding line of the roofs above the banquet hall creates a successful effect of outdoor perspective.

Qui les veist troter et courre
Verlet aporter tapis escourre
Hiraut crier et ramonner
Et lun a lautre raisonner
Francoys, breton alemant
Lombart angloys ot et normant
Et maint autre divers langage
Cestoit a oir droite rage
Qui dautre part veist pignier
Pour contoyer aiguier
Valles trenchans et eaulz purer
Et pour leur mestre pain parer
Faire taillours demander napes
Et de leur mains oster les rapes
Lun seoir lais lautre troter
Et lautre ses crotes froter
Laver et netoier leur mains
A lun plus et alautre mains
Ainçoys quon alast asseoir
Estoit merveilles a veoir
Car il menoient mult grant noise
Aussi com chascun crie et noise
Faites tost la messe est chantee
Et liaue est pieca cornee
Quant en ot chante tout avant
Chascuns ala a son retrait
Qui dust son corset desvestir
Pour le sercot ouvert vestir
Comment lamant fu
Au disner sa dame.

PLATE 26

GUILLAUME DE MACHAUT, LE DIT DU LION

fol. 103 *The Enchanted Garden*

This astonishing painting illustrates *Le Dit du Lion,* a work with a rather thin story line, which serves Machaut as a pretext for sketching a series of extremely well-observed portraits of different types of lovers. It gives the poet the opportunity to compare the true lover to the inconstant, the timid to the brazen, and to depict the amusing contrast between courtly love and the loves of peasants.

One April morning in 1342, the author is awakened by the song of birds. He arises and walks to the window of the room in the castle in which he is a guest. The window overlooks an enchanted garden, but the entrance to the garden is blocked by a stream. Machaut decides to visit this garden, but seeing neither a bridge nor a ford, he borrows a sumptuously decorated boat which he fortunately happens to come upon. He arrives at his goal, and begins to explore the garden; there he meets a lion, the symbol of the true lover, who leads him to his lady.

The scene reproduced here illustrates the two successive passages in which the garden is first seen from a distance (verses 83–106) and then from nearby (verses 189–200). On a meadow carpeted with tiny flowers, in the shade of trees that maintain the meadow's freshness, rabbits frolic and birds peck. At the edge of the forest, a number of wild animals (a wolf, a fox, a bear, and the lion who becomes the author's guide) risk vigilant glances, while a tall stag musters more courage and steps out of the woods. A stilt plover is fishing in the middle of the stream.

In his poem, Machaut praises the beauty of the trees alive with birds:

"To make their pleasing melody
Birds are sitting in a tree
One, two, five, and even six I see."

This passage is exactly rendered in the painting. All human presence has been banished from the serene vision, which shows the increased attention artists began to pay to the study of nature toward the end of the Middle Ages. This may be one of the oldest independent landscapes in European painting.

Quant la saison
d'yver decline
Et que par droit
Toute riens s'encline
Selonc nature a faire joye
Si qu'il n'est cuers
Qui ne s'esjoie
Tant assis en cuer vilain soit
Car maint l'anmeut
Et le aussi laim
Trop plus le printemps que l'yver
Car neis les bestes et li ver
Qui contre lui de la terre issent
De sa venue s'esjoissent.

Et li oysillon s'en esgaient
Qui a faire joie s'essaient
Et li paient en leur latin
Tousdis au soir et au matin
Jolement sa droite rente
Que chascuns chante ou deschante
Et face feste en sa venue
Pource qu'il a esté en mue
Car nature si leur commande
Que chascuns a chanter entende
Si que par prez et par rivages
Par plains par aunois par bocages
Par montaignes et par valees
Chantent tuit les geules trees
Si font maint son et maint bequet
Quar quant il voient le bosquet

tum suscipiant eum duo predicti epi dextera

leua qz honorifice et ipm reuerenter ducant ad ecclam canentes hoc ℟ cum canonicis p dictis Ecce mitto angelum meum qui precedat te et custodiat semper. Obserua et audi uocem meam et inimicus ero inimicis tuis et affligentes te affligam et precedet te angelus meus Finito ℟ cantetur ℣. Israel si me audieris non erit in te deus recens neqz adorabis deum alienum ego enim dominus. Obserua Cunctoqz eum populo

PLATE 27

The Coronation Book of Charles V

fol. 44v *King Charles in the Palace of the Archbishop of Reims*

The present copy of the Coronation Ceremony Book of the Kings of France was made for Charles V shortly after his own coronation; the King affixed his handwritten *ex libris* to the book, and the date: 1365. One fact is particularly noteworthy: the illustrations in the manuscript feature the King himself, with obvious concern for likeness, which is, of course, not the case in the only earlier illustrated copy of the coronation ceremony dating from the 13th century, and preserved at the Bibliothèque Nationale (Ms. Lat. 1264).

The personalization of the present volume was probably introduced at the request of the King himself, who wished to keep a record of his coronation ceremony, but it also corresponds to the overall evolution of the arts during this period, which were tending more and more toward realism and the rendering of specific detail. A similar concern with documentation is the basis for the cycle of illustrations which deal with the visit to France of Emperor Charles IV of Bohemia, depicted in the King's personal copy of the *Grandes Chroniques de France* (Plate 34). The thirty-eight paintings in the present manuscript are like a newsreel of the royal consecration, which followed the rules fixed by century-old ritual. Since the 12th century, coronations traditionally took place in Reims, with the King spending the night before the ceremony in the palace of the Archbishop of Reims. The illustration shows the King, clad in a simple tunic; the Archbishop of Reims and the Bishop of Beauvais have come to take him to the Cathedral. Outside the palace, a group of prelates and priests, preceded by two acolytes, awaits the King's arrival.

The style of the painter is decidedly derivative of the master of *Le Remède de Fortune*. However, this disciple, who worked for Charles V until the end of his reign, cannot equal his master, whose details he imitates (as in the receding roof lines behind the crenelles of the palace) without being able to create a convincing impression of space.

PLATE 28

THE CORONATION BOOK OF CHARLES V

fol. 64 *King Charles Receives the Kiss of his Peers*

After the solemn coronation, which ended with the ritual unction, the King, followed by the twelve peers, mounted a tribune which had been especially erected inside the cathedral, and took his seat on the throne. At that point he received the kiss of the peers, beginning with the Archbishop of Reims, the first among them, who had to call out three times: *Vivat rex in eternum.* Mounting the tribune was a harking back to the days of the Franks, when the King was lifted and carried on a shield by four warriors, so that the soldiers could acclaim their elected ruler.

Charles V is sitting on the throne in the middle of the tribune, which has been hung with precious draperies; he is holding the emblems of royalty, the sceptre and the *main de justice,* while receiving the kiss of the Archbishop of Reims. The latter is holding a scroll on which the ritual words have been inscribed. The other peers surround the King, holding the crown above his head. Several of the peers are recognizable by their heraldic devices: The Duke of Bourbon, the King's brother-in-law, can be seen on the left of the King, and to his extreme left, the Bishop of Beauvais. Behind the Archbishop of Reims one can recognize the King's brother, the Duke of Anjou, who is holding the coronation sword. The royal sceptre has been depicted in great detail: it looks very much like the so-called sceptre of Charlemagne in the Louvre, which must have been made for Charles V's coronation, and not toward the end of his reign, as had been assumed for a long time.

As in the preceding miniature, the artist has obviously little understanding of perspective: the feet which support the tribune are all on the same plane, and the steps of the stairs are laid down horizontally. Moreover, the incline of the pavement contradicts the angle of the altar, shown on the right side of the painting.

pia mater orationis exauditione confirma.
Habemus et nos apud te sancte pater dominum
saluatorem. qui pro nobis manus suas
tetendit in cruce per quem etiam precamur al
tissime. ut eius potentia suffragante. univer
sorum iustum frangatur impietas. populusque
tuus cessante formidine te solum timere con
sistat. Per eundem etc. Hiis expletis archiepiscopus
cum paribus coronam sustentantibus regem taliter

insignitum et deductum in solium sibi preparatum
sericis stratum et ornatum ubi collocabunt eum in sede

PLATE 29

Guillaume de Machaut, Poetic Works

fol. E *Nature Introduces her Children to the Poet*

Two paintings were added at the beginning of the manuscript: These were definitely done in Paris, by one of the main illuminators of Charles V's time, an artist traditionally known by the fitting nickname *Maître aux Boqueteaux.* The two miniatures are done in *demi-grisaille* and seem to account for the subjects which inspired the poet. The first of the two shows Nature, desirous "of revealing and exalting the good and the honors which exist in love," introducing her children to the poet to help him invent new fables of love. Nature's children are: Sense, Rhetoric, and Music.

Machaut receives Nature and her children standing outside his house, wearing a religious habit and a tonsure to recall his religious station. Behind the group rises a charming country landscape with much picturesque detail: a duck pond, peasants carrying their grain to the mill, hamlets and calvary crosses. However, the spatial arrangement of the different elements which compose the scene do not match the artist's ambitions: the main figures, Machaut, Nature, and her children, have been dropped to the bottom of the painting, pushed against the landscape which gives a theater-curtain-like effect. The horizon of the landscape itself still rises very high in the painting. There is, however, one new important factor: the abstract background which usually decorates illuminations of this period has been replaced by a real sky with clouds.

Cõment nature voulant orendroit plus que onques mes reveler ⁊ faire essaucier les biens ⁊ honneurs qui sont en amours vient a Guille de machaut ⁊ li ordene ⁊ encharge a faire sur ce nouueaux dis amoureux. et li baille pour li conseillier ⁊ aidier a ce faire trois de ses enfans. Cest asavoir Sens. Retorique ⁊ musique. et li dit par ceste maniere.

Je nature par qui tout est fourme
Quanque a ca jus ⁊ sur terre ⁊ en mer
Vieng ci a toy Guille qui fourme
T'ai a part pour faire par toy fourmer
Nouueaux dis amoureux plaisans
Pour ce te bail ci trois de mes enfans
Qui t'en donront la pratique
Et se tu nes deulz trois bien cognoissans
Nomme sont Sens. Retorique ⁊ musique

PLATE 30

GUILLAUME DE MACHAUT, POETIC WORKS

fol. D *Love Introduces his Children to the Poet*

After listening to the discourse held by Nature, it is Love's turn to introduce three of his children to Guillaume de Machaut. They are Sweet Thought, Charm, and Hope, and will "supply him with the material he needs to follow Nature's orders," according to the explanation in the corresponding heading.

Love can be recognized by his wings. Elegantly clad in brocade, and, like Nature, crowned, he leads his son, Sweet Thought, to Machaut. The son is a fashionable young man, whose padded shirtfront accentuates his narrow waistline. Charm and Hope follow close by; both are dressed in clinging robes and are wearing the hairstyles that were fashionable during Charles V's reign. In keeping with the privilege of the aged, Machaut receives his elegant visitors sitting in his study.

Behind these various figures rises a landscape that is similar to the one on the preceding page, and there is also a similar discrepancy as to the perspective in which the various elements of the scene are presented: some, like the figures in the front, are seen as though they were level with the ground, while others are presented haphazardly. These errors are particularly blatant in the case of the pond, which is vertical, while the ducks swimming in it appear in profile. The effect of distance, suggested by the smaller size of the background figures, is thwarted by the three hares all the way at the top of the landscape. The hares are almost as large as the horse and the peasant beneath them. Moreover, the interior in which Guillaume de Machaut is sitting shows less facility in the treatment of space than the works of the master of *Le Remède de Fortune* (Plate 25).

Comment Amours qui a ouy nature
vient a Guillaume de machaut et li
amaine trois de ses enfans cest asavoir
doux penser · plaisance · et esperance · pour
li donner matere a faire ce que nature
li a enchargie · et li dit par ceste maniere

Je suy amours qui maint cuer esbaudi
Et fai mener douce et ioieuse vie
Si ai oy · Guillaume je te di
Que nature qui tout fait par maistrie
Ta dit qua part ta voulu faire
Pour faire dis nouveaux de mō affaire
Pour ce tameine icy en pourveance
Pour toy donner matere a ce parfaire
Mes trois enfans en douce contenance
Cest doulz penser · plaisance et esperance ·

31

PLATE 31

LE SONGE DU VERGER

fol. 1v *The Churchman and the Knight Debate*

Le Songe du Verger is a treatise dealing with the relationship between ecclesiastic and secular power, in particular between the Papacy and the King of France. It was initially written in Latin, and translated into French in 1378 at the order of Charles V by one of the King's advisers who has not yet been convincingly identified.

In his foreword, the writer uses the dream fiction, a device that was popular in the Middle Ages. He has fallen asleep in a garden and has a dream in which the King appears, in the company of two ladies, respectively symbolizing spiritual power and worldly power. The ladies choose as their lawyers a churchman and a knight. The long debate between the two lawyers constitutes the content of the work.

The manuscript page reproduced here is from Charles V's personal copy. A large painting at the beginning of the volume gives a visual transcription of the argument set forth in the prologue: In a garden surrounded by trees, the author lies sleeping near a spring. Above him, the King of France, clad in a coat covered with fleurs-de-lys, is seated on a throne, between two crowned ladies. They incarnate the spiritual and the worldly powers and are respectively wearing a nun's robe and a worldly costume. All three sit listening to the debate between the churchman and the knight.

The creator of the painting (decidedly the *Maître aux Boqueteaux*) has not tried to render the features of the French King. As in the two *grisailles* of Ms. Fr. 1584 (Plates 29 and 30), the artist reveals not only his taste for depicting nature, but also his limitations where spatial representation is concerned: with its carefully separated figures, the painting is even regressive compared to the skillful arrangement of the figures in the manuscript of Guillaume de Machaut. Stretching upward, the garden appears to be seen on a vertical plane, while the persons and the trees have been positioned horizontally. Although the painting, which is set in a frame of copses surrounding the garden, offers little satisfaction from a spatial point of view, it is, nonetheless, undeniably successful on the decorative plane.

PLATE 32

The Livy of Charles V

fol. 7 *Roman History*

Livy was the most favored of all classical authors studied during the 14th century. His *Roman History* was an object of scholarly philological research by Petrarch, and Boccaccio translated it into Italian. In France, King Jean le Bon ordered one of Petrarch's correspondents, Pierre Bersuire, Prior of Saint Eloy of Paris, to do a French translation which was accomplished from 1354 to 1359. The King's interest in Roman history seems to have been prompted by pragmatism rather than by any humanistic concerns. He wished to learn from the examples of the past. The manuscript represented by the folio reproduced here is not Jean le Bon's copy, which has been lost, but another copy made for his son Charles V around 1370. Here, too, the King's favorite artist, the *Maître aux Boqueteaux,* was charged with the illustration.

This painting (f. 7) consists of nine small miniatures, in three juxtaposed rows of three. Each miniature is set inside a poly-lobed three-colored frame, an arrangement which has been mistaken as a characteristic of the manuscripts of Charles V. Without too much concern for historical veracity these scenes represent various episodes related to the beginnings of Roman history. Starting with the upper left medallion, we see: Aeneas landing at Laurentium; the shepherd Faustulus coming upon Romulus and Remus being suckled by the she-wolf; Remus seeing six vultures fly past while Romulus sees twelve; Romulus founding the city of Rome; the battle between Romulus and Remus, and death of the latter; the abduction of the Sabine women; the siege of Rome by the Sabines, and Tarpeia's betrayal; the Sabine women intervening between the Romans and the Sabines; Romulus being taken up to heaven before his soldiers.

In the lower margin, two scenes from the story of Hercules and Cacus have been drawn with a lighter brush: on the left, Cacus finds Hercules asleep, and steals several head of his cattle, which he drags backwards into a cave; on the right, Hercules kills Cacus outside the cave. This episode is not as gratuitous as it may seem at first glance. According to tradition, it is supposed to have taken place at the exact spot on which Rome was founded, as Livy reminds us in his text (I, 7). The hybrid in monk's garb at the end of a plant shoot on the left, who is holding an open book, is most likely a somewhat irreverent allusion to the translator, Pierre Bersuire, who was a Benedictine.

Ci commence le livre de titus livius translate du prieur de saint eloy de paris de latin en romans: prologue

A prince de tres souveraine excel
lence. Jehan roy de france par
grace divine. Frere pierre ber
ceure son petit serviteur prieur
a present de saint eloy de paris
toute humble reverence et subie
tion. Cest tout certain tres sou
verain seigneur que tous excellens princes de
tant comme il ont lenging plus cler voiant et de
plus noble et vive qualite de tant veulent il plus
volentiers encerchier et savoir les vertueus faiz
et les notables oeuvres des princes anciens et
les senz darmes raisons et industries par les
quelles ilz conquistrent iadis les pays et les ter
res et edifierent empires et royaumes et les
fonderent et acrurent deffendirent et gouverne
rent et tindrent par grans successions et par
longues durees afin que par semblables guises
ilz puissent les leur terres deffendre et gouverner.

Et les estranges possider et conquerre
en maniere deue grever leurs
anemis deffendre leur subgis
et aidier leurs amis. Ce fu don
ques la cause prince tres redoubte
que vous qui entre les autres pri
nces avez lengin tres noble. consi
derastes que le pueple romain entre tous autres
pueples qui par vertus de constance et de senz et
par puissance deuvres chevalereuses ont leur
armes portees en contrees estranges et conquiste
empires et royaumes pour eulz et pour les leur
ont bien este si seur tuit li souverain et li plus
excellent si comme assez appert en ce que eulz qui
au commencement furent une seule cite assez
povre et petite. seurent tant faire par armes
vertueuses continuees par senz et par labeurs
que il conquistrent la rondesce du monde.
Et que pour ce aleurs fais merveilleus pueent

Ou .xx.e chapitre il touche une diuision de lame et declare le premier membre
Ou .xxi.e il met et declare lautre membre de la diuision de lame.
Ci finent les titres des chapitres du premier liure de ethiques. Et ci apres cõmence le proheme qui contient .iii. chapitres. Ou premier chap il propose la fin et le finit de ceste science
doctrine. Il entent par art science pratique. Et par doctrine science speculatiue.
desirent. par desir naturel cõme leur fin et leur pfection et aucune foiz desire un hõme mal mais ce est pour ce que il a aucune apparence de bien.
operacions. cõme chanter ou dancier.
oeuures. cõme une maison ou un vaissel
Tout art et toute doctrine. et semblablement tout fait ou operacion et election appetent et desirent aucun bien. pour ce par loient bien les anciens en disant ainsi bie est ce q̃ toutes clos desirent.
Et semble quo il est difference de fins car les unes fins sont les operacions. les autres sont aucunes oeuures. ou choses faites hors les operacions ou facons et ces oeuures sōt meilleurs

PLATE 33

ARISTOTLE'S ETHICS

fol. 2v *Dedication Scene; The King and his Family; Two Scenes of Instruction*

The works of Aristotle, which had previously been accessible only to a minority of intellectuals and university scholars who read Latin, found a new public toward the end of the 14th century when Charles V ordered an important translation in 1370 from his adviser Nicole Oresme, Dean of the Chapter of Rouen. As a reward for his labors the Dean was made Bishop of Lisieux in 1377.

The King's choice had fallen upon three treatises by the Greek philosopher: Ethics, Politics, and Economics, of particular interest to a sovereign concerned with high moral standards and "good government." Two copies of this translation, both in two volumes, but of different formats, were executed for the King. One of the illustrations which appears at the beginning of the translation of the treatise on Ethics in the large-format copy clearly reveals the concerns of an enlightened monarch such as Charles V.

Divided into four three-colored four-lobed medallions, the painting starts on the upper left with a dedication scene: Charles V, wearing a simple "skull cap," is seated beneath a cone-shaped canopy, graciously accepting the manuscript from the hands of Nicole Oresme who is kneeling before him. There is a feeling of intimacy in this scene which lacks ostentation and solemnity. Charles V again appears in the next medallion, this time accompanied by Queen Jeanne de Bourbon and three of their children: the Dauphin Charles, his brother Louis, the future Duke of Orleans, and next to the Queen, Marie de France. This peaceful family scene seems meant to stress the thought that the dynastic continuity of the French monarchy had been assured since the belated births of the Dauphin and his brother.

The two lower images do not directly involve the King of France, but they illustrate ideas expressed by Oresme in his commentaries to the translation of the Ethics. On the left, a professor lectures an audience which includes a crown-bearing King. This scene probably refers to the passage in which Oresme declares that "knowledge of political science is of great benefit to the wise men whose task it is to govern." On the right, outside the door to a hall in which a master is teaching a class of adults, a beadle armed with a stick refuses entry to a young boy, which surprises a man, apparently the boy's father. A passage from the Ethics explains the beadle's severity: Charles V's adviser was of the definite opinion that young boys were not "a suitable audience for political teachings," because they lacked experience and common sense.

Premierement sist larcevesq̃
de Reims. Apres seoit
lempereur. Apres seoit
le Roy aintrosne ou milieu
du front de la sale. Apres
le Roy de france seoit le roy
des romains. Et avoit autant de distance
du Roy au Roy des romains cõme du
Roy a lempereur. Et avoient lempereur
le Roy et le Roy des romains chascun se
parement un ciel de drap dor borde de velu
au aus armes de france. et par dessus ceulz

PLATE 34

CHARLES V'S GRANDES CHRONIQUES DE FRANCE

fol. 473v *The Reception for Emperor Charles IV*

The *Grandes Chroniques de France* were composed at the beginning of the reign of Philippe le Hardi. They go back to the mythical origins of the Kings of France, and were regularly brought up to date during the 14th century by the monks of Saint-Denis, the official historiographers of the monarchy. Like his predecessors, Charles V took an interest in these texts. A luxury edition was copied out for him, with an added detailed account of the political events during the reign of Jean le Bon, and during his own reign. Unlike the preceding additions, this one was not written in Saint-Denis, but by someone in the King's immediate entourage, perhaps by his own chancellor Pierre d'Orgemont. Particular importance has been given to the visit to Paris in 1378 of Emperor Charles IV of Luxembourg, the King's maternal uncle. The detailed report of this revered visit is accompanied by a series of miniatures which illustrate its highlights.

The image shown here depicts one of the most splendid moments of the Emperor's visit: the sumptuous reception given for him by his nephew in the grand hall of the Palais de la Cité. The three principal actors of the scene, the bearded Emperor, who is recognizable by his closed-in crown, the King of France, and Venceslas, the Emperor's oldest son, are grouped beneath three canopies, decorated with fleurs-de-lys. They are at a table in the company of three prelates, while a short play which recalls the siege and the conquest of Jerusalem by Godefroy de Bouillon takes place on the right. On the left, spilling over the frame of the miniature, a vessel flying three flags with the Arms of England, Auvergne, and Flanders, symbolizes the fleet of the Crusaders. Its only passenger, a monk clad in black, probably represents Peter the Hermit, the preacher of the first Crusade.

The seductive color scheme of the entire scene does not conceal the artist's lack of a coherent spatial concept: the effect of depth is annulled by the red, gold-checkered background against which the scene stands out. The table and its guests seem suspended in mid-air. Another mistake in perspective is the size of the actors in the play: although placed in the foreground, they are smaller than the personages behind the table, probably in order to underline the differences in their stations. Compared to the banquet appearing in the manuscript of Guillaume de Machaut, Ms. Fr. 1586 (Plate 25), some thirty years earlier, this miniature appears regressive.

PLATE 35

Charles V's Grandes Chroniques de France

fol. 3v *The Coronation of Charles VI*

This beautiful page, which appears at the beginning of Charles V's volume of the *Grandes Chroniques de France,* must have been added shortly after the King's death, because it obviously pictures the coronation of his young son, Charles VI, who was crowned in Reims on September 16, 1380.

The artist has chosen the high point of the ceremony, the moment when the King of France has ascended the tribune and is being acclaimed by the twelve peers. They are divided into a lay and an ecclesiastic group, and are holding the crown above the head of their new sovereign. A group of spectators and a beadle with raised head have gathered under the tribune to watch this historical moment. On the right, another beadle seems to be discussing the event with a man dressed like a counsellor. The costumes of the participants have been treated in tones of gray, with the exception of the young King, who is draped in an ample blue coat decorated with fleurs-de-lys.

It is interesting to compare the layout of this painting with the corresponding scene in *The Coronation Book of Charles V* (Plate 28). The artist of the *Grandes Chroniques* has sacrificed the effect of "distance" adopted by the master of *The Coronation Book.* The tribune is no longer seen in a spatial context, but fills the entire scene. Nor is the spatial arrangement of the tribune particularly successful: all the actors are placed on the same vertical plane, without any depth effect. It requires a certain effort to recognize the strangely twisted thing in the lower part of the painting that looks like a screw from a wine press as the stairway leading to the tribune.

The artist is an accomplished draftsman, more at ease with the details of costume and anatomy of each of his personages, which he has drawn with a vivid pen. Together with the *Maître aux Boqueteaux* and the illustrator of *The Coronation Book,* this able but superficial illuminator was one of the artists whom Charles V employed most frequently during the last ten years of his reign.

PLATE 36

The Bible Historiale of Jean de Vaudetar

fol. 2 *Presentation to the King*

This *Bible Historiale* was given to Charles V by his adviser Jean de Vaudetar. It begins with a famous dedication scene, executed in 1371 by the painter of the King, John of Bruges, as we're informed in an inscription in gold letters on the opposite page: *(. . . et Johannis de Brugis pictor regis . . . fecit hanc picturam propria sua manu)*. It is the only preserved autographed painting by this important artist, who appeared in the King's service from 1368 on, under the name Jean Bandol of Bruges.

Kneeling before the King, Jean de Vaudetar presents him with the Bible which he had commissioned. The costumes of the two personages are treated in tones of gray, and accentuated by the green flagstone floor and the blue drapery decorated with fleurs-de-lys which hangs on the back wall. Seen as though through the arcade with slender columns framing the scene, the painting, with its flagstones in perspective, is a return to the Siennese formula which Panofsky has called "an interior by implication." The golden frame which encloses the picture is a real *trompe-l'oeil* and adds an unexpected tactile dimension.

The painting rather distinctly reveals two sources of Bandol's culture: one is essentially French and finds its expression in his clear and simple composition, in the orderly flow of the folds of the royal coat, and in the use of tones of gray; the other is of truly Flemish origin and is expressed by the artist's sharpness of vision, by his capacity to evoke the physical materiality of beings and objects (the subtle light which enlivens the King's eye, the wood of his armchair, the transparent snood of his cap, and the marbled stone of the corner of the arcade) thanks to an incomparable skill with the brush. All of these details, together with his intuition for space, reappear in Flemish painting during the next century. There is, in our opinion, an insurmountable gap in quality between this genuine painter and the contemporary French illuminators who have often been linked with him (especially the *Maître aux Boqueteaux*).

PLATE 37

THE BREVIARY OF CHARLES V

fol. 261 *Psalm 109*

Although this Breviary appears in the 1380 inventory of Charles V's property, nothing proves that it was executed for the King rather than for his father, Jean le Bon, except for one iconographic point and the style, which is even more indicative. The manuscript definitely belongs to the later works of Jean Le Noir, who probably created these illuminations after *The Hours of Yolande of Flanders* (which was completed prior to 1358, the year in which the artist entered the services of Jean le Bon and of the Dauphin) and before *The Petites Heures* of Jean de Berry, his last known work. The illustrated program of the Breviary shows the Court's attitude toward Jean Le Noir, who was considered and apparently consciously employed as a "retro" artist. A great many of the illuminations in this manuscript were copied from *The Belleville Breviary* executed some forty years earlier under Pucelle's direction (Plates 11–12). They were, however, transformed by Jean Le Noir's unmistakable style.

The illustration for Psalm 109 deserves particular attention. It is our only echo of a similar composition in the two volumes of *The Belleville Breviary.* A small miniature in the text illustrates the beginning of the Psalm and is completed by a painting of the *Last Judgment* in the lower margin. The presence of these two scenes is justified by the text of the Psalm, which begins with the words: *Dixit Dominus domino meo: sede a dextris meis.* The *Last Judgment* is probably a faithful copy of the corresponding scene in *The Belleville Breviary,* but this is decidedly not the case of the miniature enclosed in the text, where the artist has introduced a noteworthy change, doubtless at the order of Charles V: instead of the Trinity which was supposed to appear in this spot, we see God seated on a throne, motioning a King who is kneeling before him to come closer. The King's finely drawn head with its long profile can be easily recognized as Charles V's. The thoroughly audacious idea expressed in this image, which stresses the privileged relationship between God and his foremost chosen one, the King of France, agrees perfectly with Charles V's theocratic concept of royal power.

PLATE 38

The Bible Historiale of Charles V

fol. 1 *The Pentateuch; The Historical Books; The Hagiographa; The Prophets*

This image, introducing another copy of *The Bible Historiale* made for Charles V, is treated with an unbelievable abundance of detail in the style characteristic of the illustrator of *The Breviary of Charles V,* that is to say, Jean Le Noir.

The composition is divided into four parts, grouped two by two, with a devotion scene interpolated between them, showing Charles V in prayer before the Trinity. On either side, two small personages unfurl banners with inscriptions which explain the overall program. According to the corresponding inscription, the image on the upper left is supposed to evoke "The V books of the Law of Moses," i.e., the Pentateuch. Huddled inside a cave, Moses looks up at God who appears to him on top of Mount Sinai, turning his back. The five books that lie scattered in the landscape allude to the five books of the Pentateuch. Under this unusual scene, inspired by a passage from Exodus (33, 22–23), a second composition, on three levels, evokes the Historical Books. Each of these is designated by its principal hero, with the exception of the Book of the Macchabes, represented by a battle scene. The image on the upper right relates to the Hagiographa: Solomon, to whom the Proverbs, the Ecclesiastes, and the Canticle of Canticles were attributed, is represented holding three banners next to two other figures symbolizing Wisdom and the Ecclesiastes. The last section concerns the Prophets: the six "major" prophets, David, Isaiah, Jeremiah, Baruch, Hezekia, and Daniel are shown on two levels, while twelve bearded faces in the frame represent the twelve minor prophets.

The devotion scene which has been inserted into the Biblical program recalls a certain number of similar images in which Charles V expresses his desire to incarnate the ideal ruler in constant quest of wisdom and perfection. Kneeling before an image of the Trinity, the monarch is holding a banner on which a quotation from the Psalms has been inscribed: *Bonitatem et disciplinam et scientam doce me* (Psalm 118, 66). The illustrated initial in the prologue represents the Canon Guyart des Moulins, the author of *The Bible Historiale,* sitting at a desk, while another scholar looks at him in the bowl of the letter. A bearded personage, supported by two other figures, shapes the letter's vertical stem.

CI COMMENCE LI BIBLE EN FRANÇOIS

Ci comence la bible hystorial. ou les hystoires escolastres. Cest li prohemes de
celui qui mist cest livre de latin en françois

ource que li diables qui
chascun iour empesche
destourbe et enordist
les cuers des hommes
par oiseuse et par [illegible]
laz qu'il a tendu pour
nous prandre et entrer en nos cuers.
comme cil qui onques ne cesse de guerr-
oier et comment il nous puisse mener a pechie pour nos ames traire en son puant enfer avec lui. Est il necessai-
re a nous clers et prestres de sainte
eglise qui devons estre lumiere du
monde. que nous apres nos heures et
nos oroisons entendiens a aucune
bone euvre faire [illegible] le pris des armes

nez le deable. Quant il nous vient assaillir de ses ordes temptations. ne nous
truisse oiseus. par quoi il ait achoison
de legierement entrer en nos cuers. et
nous face cheoir par pechie. premierement par pensee. Et apres par euvre.
Si devons sur toutes choses fuir oiseuse. et entendre tousiours a faire aucune bone euvre qui a dieu plaise. et au
deable soit dommage et ennuieuse. Et pour
que le diable qui pluseurs fois ma
fait pechier par oiseuse. ne me puist
iamais trouver. mais touz iours en
soignie d'aucune bone euvre qui a dieu
plaise: ai ie qui sui prestres et chanoine
de. S. pere d'aire. de la [illegible]
ment. a la loenge de dieu et de la vierge marie. et de touz sains. Et apres
au profit de touz gens qui ceste euvre

PLATE 39

The Petites Heures of Jean de Berry

fol. 76 *The Arrest of Christ*

It is interesting to compare *The Arrest of Christ* in *The Petites Heures*, reproduced here, to the same scene, painted almost forty years earlier by the same artist, in *The Hours of Jeanne de Navarre* (Plate 17). The short burly mold of the figures in the older manuscript has become somewhat more elongated in *The Petites Heures.* The pictorial execution has lost some of its compactness, but has gained in size and in lightness; the color has lost some of its intensity, but has become enriched with new, careful shadings (the delicately pale yellow of Judas's robe, and the green tunic of Malchus). Nonetheless, Le Noir remains true to himself in his quest for expression, in his caricature of humanity, and his taste for the picturesque. He is almost completely liberated from Pucelle's example which he was still following in *The Hours of Jeanne de Navarre,* and of which only the motif of the soldier looking sideways out from under the raised visor of his helmet is a distinct borrowing. His composition is an original, lyrically rhythmic creation, with undeniably admirable discoveries, such as Judas's insinuatingly crafty movement as he kisses Christ, or the figure of Malchus who has become a hideous gnome writhing in pain.

All the metallic elements of the soldiers' weapons have been treated in gold and silver. The scene stands out against a background with red monochrome motifs, which rival those of *The Psalter of Bonne de Luxembourg* (Plate 18).

Two other scenes accompany this image: the illustrated initial shows *Christ on Mount Olivet;* in the lower margin, Judas refuses the money for his betrayal with which the Jews decide to buy "the potter's field." As in the Arsenal *Bible Historiale* (Plate 38), the artist demonstrates his skill with small-scale subjects.

PLATE 40

THE TRÈS BELLES HEURES OF JEAN DE BERRY *(Paris fragment)*

page 189 *Caiaphas Interrogates Christ*

A study of this fragment of *The Très Belles Heures* of Jean de Berry discloses that it had been the object of several successive campaigns of illustration during the time it belonged to the Duke. The painting reproduced here belongs to the original campaign. Like all illuminated pages in Books of Hours, the present illustration contains three distinct elements: a large painting preceding the text, an illustrated initial, and a scene at the bottom of the page.

A typically Parisian frame consisting of plant shoots encases the three scenes. Half-figures of angels, and two birds, appear in the margin. The main scene represents Christ's interrogation by Caiaphas. Firmly held in place before the high priest by two grimacing guards, Christ admits to being the Son of God. The scandalized Caiaphas tears his robe. This scene is enriched by a detail which appears only in the Gospel of Saint John (18, 22): one of the guards slaps Christ's face for his insubordinate answer to Caiaphas. The illustrated initial shows *The Derision of Christ.* The scene in the lower margin seems to represent Christ before Annas, Caiaphas' father-in-law.

There is an obvious difference in the quality of these two last images and that of the main painting. The latter, as is true of all those that were done during the first campaign of illustrations, is not the work of a simple illuminator, but of a painter whose style permits us to identify him with the creator of the famous *Parement de Narbonne.* As in the *Parement,* the scene of *The Très Belles Heures* stands out by the calm order of its composition, and by the absence of pathos in the expressions of passion. This points to an artist of classical temperament and French training, in the tradition of Pucelle.

eus in adiutorium meum intende
Domine ad adiuuandum me
festina.
Gloria patri.